ASIA-PACIFIC COUNTRIES WITH SPECIAL NEEDS DEVELOPMENT REPORT 2018

Sustainable Development and Sustaining Peace

UNITED NATIONS
ESCAP
Economic and Social Commission for Asia and the Pacific

ASIA-PACIFIC COUNTRIES WITH SPECIAL NEEDS DEVELOPMENT REPORT 2018

Sustainable Development and Sustaining Peace

Shamshad Akhtar
Executive Secretary

Hongjoo Hahm
Deputy Executive Secretary

Hamza Ali Malik
Director, Macroeconomic Policy and Financing for Development Division

United Nations publication
Sales No. E.18.II.F.15
Copyright © United Nations 2018
All rights reserved
ISBN: 978-92-1-120779-8
e-ISBN: 978-92-1-363323-6
Print ISSN: 2520-6435
Online ISSN: 2520-6443
ST/ESCAP/2831

Photo credits:
Cover: Shutterstock/LittlePerfectStock
Chapter 1: United Nations/Helena Mulkerns
Chapter 2: Shutterstock/Prazis Images
Chapter 3: Shutterstock/Sk Hasan Ali
Chapter 4: Shutterstock/Rawpixel.com

FOREWORD

Founded against the backdrop of saving "succeeding generations from the scourge of war", the United Nations has been playing an important role in preventing conflict and sustaining peace around the world. Yet, while the international community has largely been successful in reducing the incidence of war between countries, an increasing number of armed conflicts are taking place within countries. This rise is disconcerting, as armed conflict can unravel development gains and pose severe impediments to the pursuit of the Sustainable Development Goals by 2030.

The preamble to the 2030 Agenda for Sustainable Development reminds us that *"there can be no sustainable development without peace and no peace without sustainable development"*. Reflecting upon this, the 2018 edition of the *Asia-Pacific Countries with Special Needs Development Report* examines the importance of sustainable development and sustaining peace. The countries with special needs, which represent the majority of ESCAP members, are among the most vulnerable countries in the world due to the significant structural impediments to development that they face. These impediments include, inter alia, remoteness and isolation from world markets for landlocked developing countries and small island developing States, and a lack of productive capacities in least developed countries. While not all countries with special needs are ravaged by conflict or face the threat of falling into conflict,

the significant resource constraints and limited capacities that confront many of these economies – in combination with their structural challenges – translate into a higher degree of fragility and susceptibility to conflict in those countries. At the same time, these countries are less capable of coping with conflict than are other developing countries. This report therefore serves to highlight, as the first of its kind, economic, social and environmental policies that can help to achieve sustainable development and to sustain peace.

This report underlines the fact that conflict risks in countries with special needs are rooted in a variety of factors, ranging from poverty to inequalities in opportunities, resources, migration and climate change. Since these risk factors are multidimensional, risk mitigation must also be multidimensional in nature. In this context, inclusive development is a powerful tool for prevention. Investing in basic provisioning of public social services, promoting social cohesion and diversity, providing equal opportunities across different ethnic groups, enhancing the meaningful participation of women in decision-making, and addressing grievances arising from migration – both internal and international – can be effective in sustaining peace and ensuring that development is sustainable. Countries with special needs often suffer from weak institutions; therefore, improved government accountability – with revenue transparency and expenditure scrutiny – and the fair use of resource income for development and security will also be useful in reducing conflict risks.

Implementing the policy recommendations given in this report will require effective mechanisms of financing for peace. While public finance, including tax policy and public expenditure management, will be vital for sustaining peace, this report notes that in many countries with special needs official development assistance will continue to play an important role in financing sustainable development. This is especially the case for countries that exhibit high-risk levels of descending into conflict, as they are typically even more constrained by low levels of domestic resources.

The responsibility for preventing conflict from becoming violent lies primarily with national Governments. However, international and regional organizations have an important role to play in contributing to the process of preventing conflict and building peace. They can provide a vital coordination mechanism for analysing and mitigating risks related to conflict and crises. They can support national reconciliation processes and sustain peace. They can also help in preventing any potential spillover of intrastate conflict to neighbouring countries and further afield.

As always, ESCAP stands ready to assist member States in their endeavour to strengthen sustainable development, including by addressing the root causes of conflict and sustaining peace.

Shamshad Akhtar
Under-Secretary-General of the United Nations and
Executive Secretary, United Nations Economic and
Social Commission for Asia and the Pacific

EXECUTIVE SUMMARY

Peace is a necessary requirement for achieving sustainable development. Countries that sustain peace and mitigate the risks of conflict tend to be more developed than countries that are affected by conflict. Sustainable economic, social and environmental development and peace are mutually reinforcing. In contrast, conflict impedes economic activity and harms social development. Socio-economic vulnerabilities further heighten the propensity for conflict such that conflict-affected countries can easily spiral into more intense conflict. Consequently, conflict delays and inhibits progress towards the Sustainable Development Goals.

The 2030 Agenda for Sustainable Development offers a holistic framework for sustaining peace by offering an integrated architecture for tackling the root causes of conflicts. Harnessing the synergies and complementarities across the 2030 Agenda contributes to the type of holistic development that nudges nations on an upward trajectory of durable peace and sustainable development.

This report provides an integrated framework to better understand the multidimensionality of conflict and its link to the three dimensions of sustainable development. It recommends that forward-looking and coordinated regional efforts should be at the heart of finding lasting solutions.

Economic costs of conflicts exceed $1 trillion a year globally

The incidence of conflicts is increasing in the Asia-Pacific region, and cross-country analysis indicates that these events have a negative impact on human lives and economic outcomes. Conflicts unravel development and are extremely costly in human terms. In 2015, armed conflicts alone claimed 167,000 lives, and caused economic costs of more than $1 trillion globally; a striking imbalance to the $7.86 billion the United Nations'

received for its 15 peacekeeping operations for the 2016/2017 fiscal period.

Countries with special needs are less capable of coping with conflict than other developing countries

Risk levels and root causes of armed conflict vary considerably across the region, ranging from the relatively low-risk Central Asian landlocked developing countries to the higher-risk least developed countries in South Asia. Overall, 11 countries in the Asia-Pacific region have crossed the high-risk threshold of the Index for Risk Management (INFORM). Of these, only five are countries with special needs (Afghanistan, Bangladesh, Myanmar, Nepal and Papua New Guinea). Meanwhile, countries with special needs, such as Bhutan, Kazakhstan, Turkmenistan, Uzbekistan and many small island developing States, are classified as low risk. Yet, the unique structural impediments to development that countries with special needs face, coupled with their particular resource and capacity constraints, make these countries more fragile and susceptible to conflict than other developing countries.

Conflict is more likely to be triggered when multiple risk factors converge

Among the risk factors that can lead to armed conflict are a high incidence of poverty, inequalities in income, lack of employment opportunities and chronic landlessness, particularly in rural, poorer regions and marginalised communities. In turn, conflict perpetuates poverty by destroying physical and human capital and by impeding investment and innovation. Although extreme poverty and income inequality do not trigger conflict, they can increase its likelihood. Indeed, four out of five conflict incidents in countries with special needs have occurred in six States with poverty rates above 10 per cent.

Inequalities of opportunities in employment, access to health, education and other basic social services are also risk factors, especially those across culturally defined groups. Such inequalities reduce social cohesion, weaken political institutions and lead to instability. Expansion of inequality of opportunities has contributed to the growing influence of extremist groups, especially among youth. Gender-based violence is a particularly disturbing manifestation of women's inequality in several small island developing States, among others, where studies have revealed high levels of domestic violence and child abuse.

Further risk factors include politicization of ethnic divisions, international migration, natural resource abundance and scarcity, vulnerability to natural disasters and climate change. For example, most conflicts in countries with special needs have an element of ethnicity, often compounded by conflicting economic incentives across social and political groups. Such ethnicity-related conflicts are usually characterized by structural divisions between geographic regions or ethnic or religious groups, coinciding with income inequality or inequality of opportunities.

International migration can have both a positive and a negative impact on the potential for conflict. It can reduce that potential for a negative impact in countries of origin where population growth is rapid or where employment opportunities are insufficient. It can also alleviate pressures for conflict by reducing poverty through remittances, as is the case in several countries with special needs. However, significant migration within a country (such as through urbanization) and international migration can also act as risk factors for conflict by increasing pressures on social and physical infrastructure and by sparking concerns over integration and competition for resources. Similarly, while natural resource abundance can foster development due to potential revenue streams, conflict can arise from competition over resources or unfair distribution of rents. Indeed, natural resource rents in countries classified as high risk are significantly higher than in other countries, with natural-resource dependency having increased in high-risk countries during the past three decades. Exploiting scarce natural resources, such as water, can pose an additional risk of conflict as tensions surrounding access to water in North and Central Asia have shown. Risk factors do not, however, always cause conflict. Rather, they increase the likelihood of violent conflict, particularly when multiple risk factors converge. Conflict is usually triggered by certain events. These include, for example, political instability domestically and in neighbouring countries, natural disasters, climate change and economic shocks. Many countries with special needs, especially small island developing States, are highly vulnerable to extreme weather-related events. Indeed, 7 of 10 conflict incidents in Asia and the Pacific occurred within areas of earthquake hazard faults and 8 of 10 incidents occurred within drought-affected areas. This association exists partly because disasters trigger conflict risks originating from poverty and inequality, since it is often the poor who live in disaster-prone areas and are therefore most likely to lose their livelihoods as a result of disasters. In addition, conflicts can easily spill over and have a significant impact on the development of neighbouring countries, such as instability in Myanmar and in Afghanistan that has affected neighbouring countries.

The quality of governance determines whether conflicts become destructive

Bridging conditions ultimately explain why violent conflicts are triggered in some countries and not in others with similar risk factors. Among these bridging conditions is good governance, which is critical to sustaining peace. Thus, violent conflict tends not to take place if a country has a framework of viable rules that govern, for example, the allocation of resources and a settlement mechanism of potential grievances. In contrast, poor governance, weak institutions and widespread corruption magnify the likelihood of conflict being triggered by diminishing a Government's ability to resolve disputes over socio-economic risks as well as its ability to facilitate compromise between competing factions by being unable to ensure enforcement of commitments made to sustain peace.

RECOMMENDATIONS

Peace and development are intertwined. Thus, an integrated pursuit of economic, social and environmental policies, and institutional strengthening constitute integral components of the set of solutions for achieving the twin objectives of sustainable development and sustaining peace. Shaping solutions requires sustained and concerted actions by national Governments. Specific actions related to decent employment, inclusiveness and financing, which can directly minimize the risks of conflict, are necessary.

Given the economic and political interconnectedness and interdependence between and among countries, the international community, international and regional development organizations and partners play an important role in (a) supporting national reconciliation processes and sustaining peace, and (b) avoiding potential spillover of intrastate conflict to neighbouring countries and further afield.

National policies for human development, employment and equality are crucial

Employment policies are particularly important for conflict prevention. While the linkages between conflict and employment are complex and multifaceted, any sustainable solution for conflict prevention and durable peace must incorporate the role of active labour market programmes and policies, especially in creating opportunities for youth employment and improved incorporation of women into the labour force. This is particularly relevant in countries that are witnessing a youth bulge.

Governments also need to strengthen investment in human development. Better quality of education and better access to health care will contribute to higher levels of development, while equal access creates the opportunity to prosper for all, thus reducing income and social inequalities. Policies should strive for universal, adequately funded health-care systems, and provide free and universal primary and secondary education. The availability and quality of social public services should be uniform across rural and urban areas and across affluent and impoverished areas. Importantly, discrimination of ethnic and religious minorities in the labour market and in accessing public services must be prevented. Policies should support incoming populations by providing necessary basic socio-economic services.

Mitigation of conflict risks associated with natural resources requires better governance, particularly in the context of transparency and accountability in resource management. Governance in resource-rich countries can be improved by, for example, establishing fiscal rules to report, manage and use revenues from natural resources, giving special attention to mitigating the social and environmental impacts of extractive projects. In countries with scarce and diminishing resources, a system of checks and balances in Governments can mitigate risks of commitment problems associated with intertemporal inconsistency of public policy. The system should also ensure enforcement of legal frameworks as well as a transparent process for defining property rights and access to resources.

Implementing the above policy recommendations requires effective mechanisms for financing for peace. Adequate public finance, comprising both tax policy and public expenditure management, plays an important role in countries with special needs, as in many of these economies the private sector is at a nascent stage of development. While sufficient expenditure in social sectors could mitigate risks of humanitarian crises and disasters, tax policies need to mitigate the growing scourge of inequality. At the same time, building more effective, efficient and accountable tax systems must remain a top priority in view of the low level of tax revenue in many countries with special needs. For countries with sizable populations living abroad, and where remittances are particularly significant, reducing the cost of remittances to countries with special needs is important, while diaspora bonds may provide important additional sources of public finance. Generating additional funds by catalysing private capital and expertise is also critical, given that the demand for resources is much larger in countries with special needs than in other developing States, especially with regard to closing the existing infrastructure gap.

However, while strengthening domestic resources remains important for sustainable development in countries with special needs, official development assistance (ODA) plays a critical role in many of these economies, and especially those exhibiting high risk of descending into conflict, as these are typically even more resource constrained. Yet, the current context of volatile and fragmented ODA is not conducive to peace-building. In addition to increasing ODA and honouring long-held commitments to development cooperation, as emphasised in the Addis Ababa Action Agenda, international partners must focus on streamlining ODA flows, and enhancing synergies among each other in order to prevent conflict and relapses. In particular, ODA should be aligned more closely to the twin objectives of building strong foundations that minimize risk factors of conflict and fostering institutional conditions to secure peace.

The supporting role of the international community is essential

As confrontations today primarily take the form of intrastate conflicts, efforts to build and sustain peace must be nationally-driven, with the responsibility for identifying, driving and directing priorities, strategies and activities resting with national Governments. However, given the economic and political interconnectedness and interdependence between and among countries, and considering that risk factors can spill over to neighbouring economies and that conflicts can have transboundary impacts, the international community, international and regional development organizations and partners also play an important role in supporting national reconciliation processes and sustaining peace. This can be achieved by enhancing regional economic cooperation and integration, and supporting South-South development cooperation, with a focus on the countries with special needs. Greater cooperation in particular is necessary when addressing the growing challenges of adaptation to climate change and to reducing shared vulnerabilities to the increasing environmental risks. Moreover, this will further build confidence and trust between countries, thereby reducing the risk of interstate conflict.

The international community also plays a vital role in preventing conflict and building peace through analytical research on drivers of conflict as well as on underlying causes of vulnerability and their linkage to the Sustainable Development Goals. They can also contribute to strengthening capacities in member States, particularly in countries with special needs, to formulate and implement policies that assess risks and costs of vulnerabilities to conflict. Finally, through their intergovernmental structure, they can provide a platform for addressing conflict prevention at the regional and subregional levels and by supporting an exchange of lessons learnt, and methods and best practices across countries for providing peer-learning opportunities.

ACKNOWLEDGEMENTS

This report was prepared under the overall direction and guidance of Shamshad Akhtar, Under-Secretary-General of the United Nations and Executive Secretary of the Economic and Social Commission for Asia and the Pacific. Hongjoo Hahm, Deputy Executive Secretary, provided valuable advice and comments. The report was coordinated by a core team under the direction of Hamza Ali Malik, Director of Macroeconomic Policy and Financing for Development Division. The core team, led by Oliver Paddison, included Sudip Ranjan Basu, Andrzej Bolesta, Nyingtob Pema Norbu and Yusuke Tateno.

ESCAP staff who contributed substantively include: Shuvojit Banerjee, Jose Antonio Pedrosa Garcia, Zhenqian Huang, Alberto Isgut, Zheng Jian, Daniel Jeongdae Lee, Vatcharin Sirimaneetham, Gabriela Spaizmann and Tientip Subhanij of the Macroeconomic Policy and Financing for Development Division; Hong Peng Liu (Director) and Kohji Iwakami of the Energy Division; Stefanos Fotiou (Director) and Ram Tiwaree of the Environment and Development Division; Tiziana Bonapace (Director) and Syed Ahmed of the Information and Communications Technology and Disaster Risk Reduction Division; Yanhong Zhang and Christopher Lovell of the Statistics Division; Nagesh Kumar (Director), Therese Bjork, Grace Puliyel, Marco Roncarati, Ermioni Sokou, Vanessa Steinmayer, and Paul Tacon of the Social Development Division; Mia Mikic (Director) and Marcel Proksch of the Trade, Investment and Innovation Division; Adnan Aliani (Director) and Chrispin Kapinga of the Strategic Programme Management Division; Sangmin Nam (Officer-in-Charge) and Nobuko Kajiura of the ESCAP Subregional Office for East and North-East Asia; Hirohito Toda (Head), Nikolay Pomoshikov and Hiroaki Ogawa of the ESCAP Subregional Office for North and Central Asia; Iosefa Malavfa (Head), Sanjesh Naidu and Anna Naupa of the ESCAP Subregional Office for the Pacific; Nagesh Kumar (Officer-in-Charge), Matthew Hammill and Wanphen Sreshthaputra-Korotki of the ESCAP Subregional Office for South and South-West Asia; Mitchell Hsieh and Lorenzo Santucci of the Office of the Executive Secretary.

The report also benefited from the discussions at the Expert Group Meeting on the regional implementation of the Istanbul Declaration and Programme of Action for least developed countries held on 6 and 8 December 2017 at ESCAP. The eminent group of policymakers, scholars and development practitioners at the Expert Group Meeting were: Rajiv Biswas, Asia-Pacific Chief Economist, IHS Markit, Singapore; Derek Brien, Executive Director, Pacific Institute of Public Policy, Vanuatu; Santi Chaisrisawatsuk, Director, Center for Development Economics Studies, National Institute of Development Administration, Thailand; Vutha Hing, Research Fellow, Cambodia Development Resource Institute, Cambodia; Kazi Anowarul Hoque, Additional Secretary, Economic Relations Division, Ministry of Finance, Bangladesh; Thida Kyu, Professor and Head, Department of Economics, Yangon University of Economics, Myanmar; Syed Nuruzzaman, International Consultant, Bangladesh; Jinhwan Oh, Associate Professor, Graduate School of International Studies, Ewha Woman's University, Republic of Korea; Selim Raihan, Professor, Department of Economics, University of Dhaka, and Executive Director, South Asian Network on Economic Modeling, Bangladesh; Posh Raj Pandey, Chairman, South Asia Watch on Trade, Economics and Environment, Nepal; Shankar Prasad Sharma, former Vice-Chairman, National Planning Commission, Nepal; Ehsan Shayegan, Founder and CEO of Porsesh Research and Studies Organization, Afghanistan; Mana Southichack, Executive Director, Lao Intergro Sole Company Limited, Vientiane, Lao People's Democratic Republic; Zulfiya Suleimenova, National Graduate Institute for Policy Studies, Japan; Tandin Wangchuk, Researcher and Manager of Outlook Consulting Service, Bhutan.

Walaiporn Laosuksri of the Macroeconomic Policy and Financing for Development Division, ESCAP, provided research assistance. Valuable inputs were also received from interns Lin Fang and Zakaria Zoundi.

The manuscript was edited and proofread by Robert A. R. Oliver. The graphic design was created by a consultant with the support and facilitation of Ricardo Dunn and Sompot Suphutthamongkhon of the ESCAP Strategic Publications, Communications and Advocacy Section. The layout and printing were provided by Clung Wicha Press.

Arpaporn Chomcherngpat, Pannipa Jangvithaya, Sukanitt Jarunveshsuti, Woranooch Thiusathien, and Sutinee Yeamkitpibul of the Macroeconomic Policy and Financing for Development Division undertook all administrative processing necessary for the issuance of the publication.

CONTENTS

CONTENTS *(continued)*

Boxes

Figures

CONTENTS *(continued)*

Tables

EXPLANATORY NOTES

Analyses in the *Asia-Pacific Countries with Special Needs Development Report 2018* are based on data and information available up to the end of March 2018.

Groupings of countries and territories/areas referred to in the present issue of the Report are defined as follows:

- Countries with special needs – least developed countries, landlocked developing countries and small island developing States.
- ESCAP region:
  - ESCAP member States – Afghanistan; Armenia; Australia; Azerbaijan; Bangladesh; Bhutan; Brunei Darussalam; Cambodia; China; Democratic People's Republic of Korea; Fiji; Georgia; India; Indonesia; Iran (Islamic Republic of); Japan; Kazakhstan; Kiribati; Kyrgyzstan; Lao People's Democratic Republic; Malaysia; Maldives; Marshall Islands; Micronesia (Federated States of); Mongolia; Myanmar; Nauru; Nepal; New Zealand; Pakistan; Palau; Papua New Guinea; Philippines; Republic of Korea; Russian Federation; Samoa; Singapore; Solomon Islands; Sri Lanka; Tajikistan; Thailand; Timor-Leste; Tonga; Turkey; Turkmenistan; Tuvalu; Uzbekistan; Vanuatu; and Viet Nam;
  - Associate members – American Samoa; Cook Islands; French Polynesia; Guam; Hong Kong, China; Macao, China; New Caledonia; Niue; and Northern Mariana Islands
- Developing ESCAP region – ESCAP region excluding Australia, Japan and New Zealand.
- Developed ESCAP region – Australia, Japan and New Zealand.
- Least developed countries – Afghanistan, Bangladesh, Bhutan, Cambodia, Kiribati, Lao People's Democratic Republic, Myanmar, Nepal, Solomon Islands, Timor-Leste, Tuvalu and Vanuatu.
- Landlocked developing countries – Afghanistan, Armenia, Azerbaijan, Bhutan, Kazakhstan, Kyrgyzstan, Lao People's Democratic Republic, Mongolia, Nepal, Tajikistan, Turkmenistan and Uzbekistan.
- Small island developing States:
  - ESCAP member States – Fiji, Kiribati, Maldives, Marshall Islands, Micronesia (Federated States of), Nauru, Palau, Papua New Guinea, Samoa, Singapore, Solomon Islands, Timor-Leste, Tonga, Tuvalu and Vanuatu;
  - Associate members – American Samoa, Cook Islands, French Polynesia, Guam, New Caledonia, Niue and Northern Mariana Islands.
- Pacific – American Samoa, Australia, Cook Islands, Fiji, French Polynesia, Guam, Kiribati, Marshall Islands, Micronesia (Federated States of), Nauru, New Caledonia, New Zealand, Niue, Northern Marina Islands, Palau, Papua New Guinea, Samoa, Solomon Islands, Tonga, Tuvalu and Vanuatu.
- Due to the limited availability of data, associate members of ESCAP are excluded from the analysis by the Report unless otherwise indicated.
- Singapore is not considered to be a small island developing State in the Report because of its high level of development and high-income status, and for simplicity of analysis.

Bibliographical and other references have not been verified. The United Nations bears no responsibility for the availability or functioning of URLs.

The designations employed and the presentation of the material in this publication do not imply the expression of any opinion whatsoever on the part of the Secretariat of the United Nations concerning the legal status of any country, territory, city or area, or of its authorities, or concerning the delimitation of its frontiers or boundaries.

Mention of firm names and commercial products does not imply the endorsement of the United Nations.

Growth rates are on an annual basis, except where otherwise indicated.

Reference to "tons" indicates metric tons.

References to dollars ($) are to United States dollars, unless otherwise stated.

The term "billion" signifies a thousand million. The term "trillion" signifies a million million.

In the tables, two dots (..) indicate that data are not available or are not separately reported; a dash (−) indicates that the amount is nil or negligible; and a blank indicates that the item is not applicable.

In dates, a hyphen (-) is used to signify the full period involved, including the beginning and end years, and a stroke (/) indicates a crop year, fiscal year or plan year.

Country or area in the ESCAP region	ISO 3166-1 Alpha-3 code	Country or area in the ESCAP region	ISO 3166-1 Alpha-3 code	Country or area in the ESCAP region	ISO 3166-1 Alpha-3 code
Afghanistan	AFG	Japan	JPN	Papua New Guinea	PNG
American Samoa	ASM	Kazakhstan	KAZ	Philippines	PHL
Armenia	ARM	Kiribati	KIR	Republic of Korea	KOR
Australia	AUS	Kyrgyzstan	KGZ	Russian Federation	RUS
Azerbaijan	AZE	Lao People's Democratic Republic	LAO	Samoa	WSM
Bangladesh	BGD	Macao, China	MAC	Singapore	SGP
Bhutan	BTN	Malaysia	MYS	Solomon Islands	SLB
Brunei Darussalam	BRN	Maldives	MDV	Sri Lanka	LKA
Cambodia	KHM	Marshall Islands	MHL	Tajikistan	TJK
China	CHN	Micronesia (Federated States of)	FSM	Thailand	THA
Cook Islands	COK	Mongolia	MNG	Timor-Leste	TLS
Democratic People's Republic of Korea	PRK	Myanmar	MMR	Tonga	TON
Fiji	FJI	Nauru	NRU	Turkey	TUR
French Polynesia	PYF	Nepal	NPL	Turkmenistan	TKM
Georgia	GEO	New Caledonia	NCL	Tuvalu	TUV
Guam	GUM	New Zealand	NZL	Uzbekistan	UZB
Hong Kong, China	HKG	Niue	NIU	Vanuatu	VUT
India	IND	Northern Mariana Islands	MNP	Viet Nam	VNM
Indonesia	IDN	Pakistan	PAK		
Iran (Islamic Republic of)	IRN	Palau	PLW		

ACRONYMS

ADB	Asian Development Bank
CSN	countries with special needs
ESCAP	United Nations, Economic and Social Commission for Asia and the Pacific
D-index	Dissimilarity index
DESA	United Nations, Department of Economic and Social Affairs
EITI	Extractive Industries Transparency Initiative
FDI	foreign direct investment
FSI	Fragile States Index
GDP	gross domestic product
GIS	geographic information systems
HAI	Human Assets Index
HDI	Human Development Index
ICT	information and communications technology
IDPs	internally displaced persons
INFORM	Index for Risk Management
LDCs	least developed countries
LLDCs	landlocked developing countries
MDGs	Millennium Development Goals
ODA	official development assistance
OECD	Organisation for Economic Co-operation and Development
OHRLLS	United Nations, Office of the High Representative for the Least Developed Countries, Landlocked Developing Countries and Small Island Developing States
PPP	purchasing power parity
PPPs	public-private partnerships
SDGs	Sustainable Development Goals
SIDS	small island developing States
SMEs	small and medium-sized enterprises
UCDP	Uppsala Conflict Data Programme
UNDP	United Nations Development Programme
UNEP	United Nations Environment Programme
UNESCO	United Nations Educational, Scientific and Cultural Organisation
UNFCCC	United Nations Framework Convention on Climate Change
WHO	World Health Organization

Introduction

The United Nations was founded in the aftermath of the unparalleled devastation inflicted by two subsequent World Wars, with the determination *"to save succeeding generations from the scourge of war, which twice in our lifetime has brought untold sorrow to mankind"*.[1] Since then, significant technological and socio-economic advances have taken place globally, with tremendous progress in development occurring particularly in the Asia-Pacific region. Indeed, with hundreds of millions of people having been lifted out of poverty in the region and significant achievements made over a broad range of social, economic and environmental development indicators, Asia and the Pacific was instrumental in meeting the first Millennium Development Goals of halving rates of extreme poverty (ESCAP, ADB and UNDP, 2017).

Marking the 100th anniversary of the end of the First World War in 2018, the world has largely been successful in reducing the incidence of war between countries (interstate conflict). However, in recent years, an increasing number of armed conflicts have taken place within countries (intrastate conflict). Such conflicts tend to last longer, are usually more violent and are more difficult to resolve. By unravelling decades of development, they mar the significant development that has taken place. They weaken institutional mechanisms, social cohesion and infrastructure, thereby posing severe impediments to the pursuit of sustainable development.

The disruptive effects of conflict on development and human wellbeing are highlighted by the fact that two-thirds of fragile countries were unable to achieve the Millennium Development Goals.[2] Indeed, just as the proportion of extreme poor living in countries affected by conflict has increased sharply, the destructive and long-lasting impact of conflict on development is demonstrated by its estimated cost, with more than 167,000 persons having lost their lives in conflict in 2015 and the economic cost of armed conflict alone reaching $1.04 trillion (Institute for Economics and Peace, 2017). This amount is more than 130 times greater than the appropriation of $7.86 billion that the United Nations made for its 15 peacekeeping operations for the 2016/2017 fiscal period.[3] Yet, with peacebuilding expenditure amounting to less than 1 per cent of the cost of conflict, more effort is required to ensure that conflict is prevented from taking place and peace is sustained.

In its boldest and most transformative agenda for humanity to date, the 2030 Agenda for Sustainable Development and its pledge to leave no one behind, the international community has recognized that peaceful, just and inclusive societies are critical to development. With its *"soaring ambition – to ensure peace and prosperity for all..."*, the agenda clearly states that *"there can be no sustainable development without peace and no peace without sustainable development"*.[4] It also explicitly includes as Goal 16 to *"promote peaceful and inclusive societies for sustainable development"*.

Conflicts are multidimensional in causes and impacts, ranging from socio-economic to environmental factors. Sustainable development, with its simultaneous emphasis on social and economic development and environmental sustainability, is therefore critical to providing a foundation for sustaining peace. This is supported by the fact that in addition to Goal 16, several targets across the 2030 Agenda are directly related to violence, justice or inclusivity, including parts of Goal 4 (inclusive and equitable quality education and lifelong learning opportunities for all), Goal 5 (gender equality and empowering all women and girls), Goal 8 (sustained, inclusive and sustainable economic growth, full and productive employment and decent work for all), Goal 10 (reducing inequality within and among countries) and Goal 11 (making cities and human settlements inclusive, safe, resilient and sustainable).

This report analyses the multidimensional linkages between sustainable development and sustaining peace by distilling cross-cutting elements. It does so with the objective of proposing a framework that links sustaining peace to sustainable development. For this, the report identifies instrumental "risk factors" that structurally increase the likelihood of conflict along with institutional "bridging conditions" and immediate "triggers" of conflict.

While peace and sustainable development reinforce each other, even when pursued jointly, social and economic development and environmental sustainability may not be sufficient to build peace and prevent conflict. Rather, political economy dynamics as well as governance and institutional mechanisms are also critical to ensuring interlinkages between sustainable development and peace.

Importantly, one must make a clear distinction between the "absence of conflict" and "durable peace". Thus, an absence of conflict does not necessarily imply that a society is operating at the frontier of peaceful conditions. Rather, the latency of conflict suggests that it is critical to address the underlying structural drivers of conflict even in the absence of conflict. Sustaining peace

requires dealing with tensions before they arise and respecting peoples' basic human rights. Once a conflict erupts it can escalate rather swiftly; an example of such a situation is Myanmar, where despite a fast-growing economy, a communal incident has flared up underlying ethnic tensions that have now assumed an international dimension with the involvement of multiple countries and international organizations.[5] Thus, assessments of conflict must *"go beyond the dichotomy on fragility, and look for dimensions of fragility that may be present even in supposedly non-fragile countries"* (UNDP, 2016b).

An analytical framework, such as that presented in figure A, is therefore helpful in understanding the link between sustainable development and sustaining peace, and in integrating development challenges to sustaining peace. This framework reflects the consensus on the relationship between peace and development, which must integrate factors beyond the immediate triggers of conflict. These factors are essentially the building blocks of sustainable development and its three pillars of social, economic and environmental development that need to be implemented through an accountable, just and transparent institutional framework. Factors that

Figure A. Linkages between sustainable development, peace and the risk factors of conflict

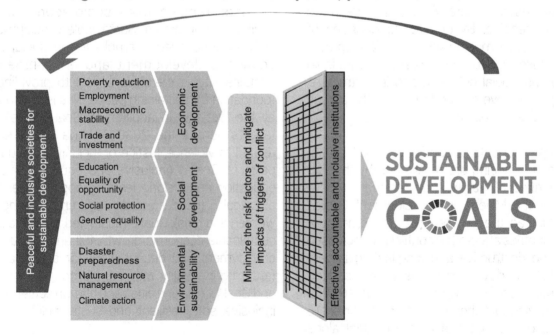

Source: ESCAP.

contribute to sustainable development minimize the risks of conflict, while conflict in turn can thwart the pursuit of the priorities required for sustainable development.[6]

Countries with special needs

This report focuses on sustaining peace in countries with special needs, which comprise least developed countries, landlocked developing countries and small island developing States. *A priori*, there is no reason why insecurity and conflict should affect countries with special needs more than other developing countries. Indeed, conflict is not confined to countries where significant development gaps exist. For instance, the Index for Risk Management (INFORM)[7], which captures exposure to natural and human-made hazards, socio-economic vulnerability and susceptibility of communities to those hazards as well as institutional and infrastructure capacities to address disasters and violent conflicts, identifies only five countries with special needs in the Asia-Pacific region alongside several other developing countries as high-risk countries. Several countries with special needs, including landlocked developing countries (Kazakhstan and Turkmenistan), a least developed country (Bhutan, which is also landlocked) and many small island developing States, are in fact classified by the Index for Risk Management (INFORM) as low risk.

Countries with special needs are, however, confronted with significant structural impediments to development. These include the lack of direct territorial access to the sea, translating into remoteness and isolation from world markets for landlocked developing countries; the geographic isolation and lack of economies of scale of small island developing States, where climate change threatens their very existence; and the lack of productive capacities, which stands out among the plethora of development challenges of least developed countries. At the same time, many countries with special needs face significant resource constraints and limited capacities. It is the resulting combination of these factors that translates into a high level of vulnerability to shocks of socio-economic or environmental nature for countries with special needs, and

which ultimately makes them more susceptible to conflict and insecurity than other developing countries in the region.

Indeed, peace and security are highlighted as guiding principles of the Istanbul Programme of Action for Least Developed Countries as well as the Small Island Developing States Accelerated Modalities of Action (SAMOA) Pathway. Peace and sustainable development are mutually reinforcing, thus calling for an integrated approach to addressing risks, security and governance. The Istanbul Programme of Action exhibits the highest degree of alignment by explicitly identifying poverty as one of the causes of conflict in least developed countries. Reducing vulnerability to natural hazards is further underscored in both the Istanbul Programme of Action and the SAMOA Pathway, recognizing that least developed countries and small island developing States bear a disproportionately heavy impact of natural hazards exacerbated by climate change. Both programmes of action also give high priority to good governance, which is essential for risk mitigation, poverty eradication and social protection, and most importantly, conflict prevention. While the Vienna Programme of Action for Landlocked Developing Countries focusses primarily on geographic constraints, it targets dimensions of peace through strengthening of regional cooperation, and emphasizes bridging socio-economic gaps and building resilience.

In addition to the programmes of action for countries with special needs, the Addis Ababa Action Agenda on Financing for Development acknowledges *"the development challenge posed by conflict, which not only impedes but can reverse decades of development gains, [...] the peacebuilding financing gap, and the importance of the Peacebuilding Fund."* Given that resource inadequacy is a binding constraint coupled with a weak institutional capacity to absorb and expend resources, underscoring the role of public finance management in such contexts is critical. Finally, the international community is placing renewed focus on the nexus of sustainable development and sustaining peace, as exemplified by recent reviews within the United Nations (box A).

Box A. Revisiting the nexus between development and peace within the United Nations

In view of the growing recognition that peace and development are interlinked, three key reviews were undertaken in 2015: (a) the United Nations Global Peace Operations Review; (b) the Peacebuilding Architecture Review; and (c) the Global Study on the Implementation of Security Council Resolution 1325 on Women, Peace and Security. These reviews noted that violent conflict is a central challenge for development, and they highlighted the importance of "sustaining peace". In April 2016, the General Assembly and Security Council thus adopted radical parallel resolutions on the review of the peacebuilding architecture.[a] By formally defining "sustaining peace" as a *"goal and process...which encompasses activities aimed at preventing the outbreak, escalation, continuation and recurrence of conflict, addressing root causes, assisting parties to conflict to end hostilities, ensuring national reconciliation, and moving towards recovery, reconstruction and development"*, these resolutions dispense with the notion that peacebuilding occurs only in post-conflict conditions; rather, they highlight the importance of peacebuilding before conflict arises in the first place. By stating that *"development, peace and security, and human rights are interlinked and mutually reinforcing"* (Security Council Resolution S/RES/2282), the international community has recognized that conflict has an impact on all three dimensions of sustainable development, and that concerted efforts at all levels are required to ensure that peace is sustained and conflict is avoided.

Overall, the resolutions represent a comprehensive statement on the role of the United Nations in peacebuilding and prevention – connecting efforts for peace and security, sustainable development and human rights. In this regard, these resolutions are fundamentally important as they realign the organization with its founding document by emphasizing the primacy of the United Nations in peacebuilding and prevention. Through the pillars of peace and security, development, and human rights, they recognize that the prevention of violence and conflict stretches beyond (short-term) intervention and post-conflict construction, and that women play a significant role in conflict resolution and sustainable peacebuilding. At the same time, the Resolutions reaffirm that efforts to build and sustain peace must be nationally-driven, and that the primary responsibility for identifying, driving and directing priorities, strategies and activities for sustaining peace lies with national Governments and authorities. They also state that *"sustaining peace is a shared task and responsibility that needs to be fulfilled by the Government and all other national stakeholders, and should flow through all three pillars of the United Nations engagement at all stages of conflict"*.

This is particularly relevant in view of the shift in the type of conflict that has taken place since the Second World War, with confrontations today primarily taking the form of intrastate conflicts involving non-state groups rather than interstate confrontations. Prevention of conflict in the twenty-first century is therefore increasingly dependent on the ability of national Governments to foster balanced development that spurs an upward spiral of mutually reinforcing peace and development outcomes.

At the same time, conflict and subsequent violence can evolve to levels that spillover to neighbouring countries, thereby taking on an international dimension, especially given the interconnected and interdependent nature of the global economy. Indeed, a conflict in one country can have consequences not only for its immediate neighbours, but even in another part of the world. Concerted efforts to tackle conflict and sustain peace at the international level are therefore needed.

[a] General Assembly Resolution A/RES/70/262 and Security Council Resolution S/RES/2282.

This report is structured as follows. Chapter 1 sets the context by providing an overview of linkages between sustainable development and peace, drawn largely from existing literature and a rapidly evolving body of associated databases. It ascertains the link between peace and conflict by referring to existing indices and the Sustainable Development Goals (SDGs). Chapter 2 describes the landscape of conflict in the Asia-Pacific countries with special needs. Chapter 3 delves into the structural dynamics of conflict by identifying risk factors, bridging conditions and triggers of conflict in an analytical framework. It explores underlying elements that increase the likelihood of conflict in order to derive policy prescriptions for a preventive framework. Chapter 4 discusses several possible recommendations, ranging from domestic economic and social policies to the role of the multilateral community, and a more fragility-sensitive refinement of the modalities of official development assistance (ODA) disbursement.

ENDNOTES

1   Preamble of United Nations Charter.

2   Fragility is commonly defined as a combination of exposure to risk and insufficient coping capacity of the State, system and/or communities to manage, absorb or mitigate those risks.

3   General Assembly Press Release GA/AB/4201.

4   See preamble of Resolution A/RES/70/1.

5   See http://www.rakhinecommission.org/app/uploads/2017/08/FinalReport_Eng.pdf.

6   A/RES/70/1 – Transforming Our World: The 2030 Agenda for Sustainable Development.

7   The Index for Risk Management (INFORM) is a collaboration of the Inter-Agency Standing Committee Task Team for Preparedness and Resilience and the European Commission. The Inter-Agency Standing Committee is an inter-agency forum involving the United Nations and non-United Nations humanitarian partners for coordination of humanitarian assistance. It was established in 1992 in response to General Assembly Resolution 46/182 to serve as the primary mechanism for inter-agency coordination relating to humanitarian assistance.

     INFORM partners include: ACAPS; the European Commission; Food and Agriculture Organization (FAO); Global Facility for Disaster Reduction and Recovery (GFDRR); Insurance Development Forum (IDF); Internal Displacement Monitoring Centre (IDMC); International Organization for Migration (IOM); United Nations Office for the Coordination of Humanitarian Affairs (OCHA); Organisation for Economic Co-operation and Development (OECD); Pacific Disaster Center; Start Network; UK Aid; United Nations Development Programme (UNDP); United Nations Department of Political Affairs (DPA); United Nations Environment Programme (UNEP); United Nations Population Fund (UNFPA); United Nations High Commissioner for Refugees (UNHCR); United Nations Children's Fund (UNICEF); United Nations International Strategy for Disaster Reduction (UNISDR); United Nations University Institute for Environment and Human Security (UNU-EHS); United Nations Entity for Gender Equality and the Empowerment of Women (UN-WOMEN), United States of America; World Food Programme (WFP); and World Health Organization (WHO). These partner agencies incorporate INFORM in their internal decision-making processes. For example, OCHA uses INFORM as one of the inputs for its funding allocation. Similarly, WFP is using INFORM to support decisions on prioritisation of emergency preparedness and resilience activities. See www.inform-index.org for more details.

CHAPTER 1

Peace and development

A. The linkages between peace and sustainable development

Peace is a necessary and foundational requirement for sustainable development. Conflict and subsequent violence containment are undeniably detrimental to the pursuit of sustainable development. Thus, the 2030 Agenda for Sustainable Development explicitly recognizes that peaceful, just and inclusive societies are a development goal and a cross-cutting theme through Goal 16 which is based on the premise that *"high levels of armed violence and insecurity have a destructive impact on a country's development, affecting economic growth and often resulting in long-standing grievances that can last for generations."*[1] Hence, *"sustaining peace is a shared task and responsibility that needs to be fulfilled by the Government and all other national stakeholders, and should flow through all three pillars of the United Nations engagement at all stages of conflict and in all its dimensions, and needs sustained international attention and assistance."*[2]

The direct and indirect costs of conflicts are significant. On the monetary front, it is estimated that in 2016 the cost of violence containment for Afghanistan and Myanmar reached a staggering 52.1 per cent and 8.4 per cent of GDP, respectively (Institute for Economics and Peace, 2017).[3] The implications of the impact of conflict on poverty are equally alarming as it is estimated that around 43 per cent of the world's poor are concentrated in countries affected by conflict or in fragile states. By 2030, these countries are projected to account for 62 per cent of the world's poorest people, even under a best-case scenario that envisages significant institutional and development improvements (OECD, 2015). Conflicts *"reflect not just a problem for development, but a failure of development"* (Collier and others, 2003). With the overriding principle of "leaving no-one behind" enshrined in the SDGs, enhancing the inclusiveness of development outcomes requires targeting vulnerable groups in conflict countries. Elimination of poverty will therefore require an unprecedented acceleration in the improvement of governance and development outcomes.

The 2030 Agenda recognizes that *"sustainable development cannot be realized without peace and security; and peace and security will be at risk without sustainable development."*[4] The SDGs offer a powerful and integrated architecture for tackling the root causes of conflicts by recognizing the interdependence between their economic, social and environmental dimensions through a range of thematic and sector-specific goals and indicators. Acknowledging the nexus between development and peace, Goal 16 calls for nurturing peaceful, just and inclusive societies to offer an environment that supports conflict prevention and allows the uninterrupted, effective and efficient implementation of sustainable development.

Evidently, countries that can sustain peace and mitigate the risks of conflict tend to achieve higher levels of development, whereas those afflicted by repeated cycles of political turmoil and violent conflicts lag behind, with their economic growth undermined and human development either regressing or stagnant. For example, the countries that have achieved high levels of socio-economic outcomes, as measured by

their Human Development Index (HDI), are also those that have sustained stable and peaceful conditions (figure 1.1). Thus, least developed countries are clustered around the right-bottom corner of the left panel of the figure, consistent with their higher levels of conflict risk. This strong relationship between human development and conflict is driven by mutually reinforcing underlying dynamics that can be conceptualized in a conflict-human development trap (Kim and Conceicao, 2010). Essentially, low HDI levels as a structural factor increase the risk of conflict; in turn, conflict can destroy economic and social capital, and consequently human development.

The strong association is also observed when assessed against environmental outcomes whereby more stable and inclusive Governments have exhibited a stronger ability to address environmental priorities (right-hand panel of figure 1.1). Conversely, various empirical studies have established robust relationships between low levels of development and higher propensities for conflict (Collier and Hoeffler, 2004).

Figure 1.1. Sustainable development and state fragility

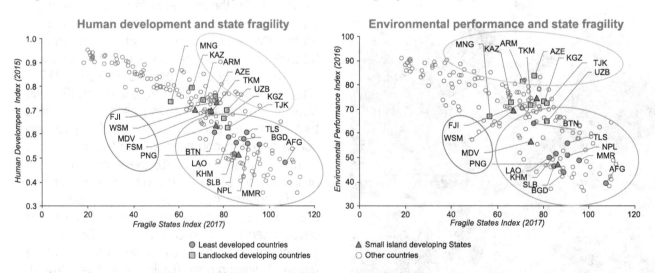

Source: ESCAP, based on the Human Development Data for 2015 from the United Nations Development Programme, the Environmental Performance Index for 2016 from Yale University, and the Fragile States Index for 2017 from the Fund for Peace. Accessed 20 November 2017.

Note: The Fragile States Index attempts to capture the vulnerability of States to collapse, based on indicators that can be broadly categorized into social, economic and political factors. While this report primarily refers to the INFORM as a comprehensive measure of risk, it may include other indices to demonstrate that the relationships are independent of the index. Country names and codes are available in the explanatory notes.

1. Empirical issues

While there is a high degree of academic consensus on the correlation between sustained peace and/or conflict prevention and sustainable development, the causal linkages have not been proven unequivocally, due to a lack of data and credible econometric methods (Blattman and Miguel, 2010). Challenges also exist due to the various national and subnational levels at which conflict occurs, which makes it difficult to establish deterministic estimates when regressed against broad aggregates. At the subnational level, cross-country models are too blunt to pick up important interactions. This is particularly relevant in today's context where conflicts are increasingly assuming an intrastate manifestation. Omitted-variable bias could also cause peace and sustainable development to move simultaneously. Explanatory factors such as low per capita income and conflict could be joint outcomes of weak political institutions (Ray and Esteban, 2017), just as country-specific historical factors are highly significant in explaining both conflict and weak institutions thereby offsetting the role of low per capita income (Djankov and Retbak-Querol, 2010).

Even the definition of conflict can be contentious at times, as parameters could only consider fatalities or could encompass other factors that characterize more developed societies.[5] This is consequential in explaining why there is no clear and robust link between inequality and conflict, as some forms of conflict are more muted while some may be expressed through civilized protests and thereby excluded from data. Moreover, available indicators may not capture factors or channels through which inequality and conflict interact. For example, the Gini coefficient of income inequality does not capture social tensions (Ray and Esteban, 2017). Alternatively, the specification of the relationship may be flawed. For example, data on ethnic fractionalization may not be sufficiently nuanced to capture channels through which diversity leads to confrontation; hence, the notion of "polarization" should be used instead (Esteban and Ray, 1994). Even within a subset of the academic discourse, such as the environment-conflict nexus, there is significant heterogeneity across estimates as diverse factors such as the political, economic, social and geographic context of a society mediates its response to climatic events (Hsiang and others, 2013). Thus, conceptual or theoretical approaches and case studies can only, at best, accompany cross-country analysis to infer the causality, but these cannot be generalized. Nevertheless, the imperative of securing a peaceful environment to facilitate socio-economic development is evident.

B. Capturing the multidimensionality and complexity of peace and conflict

1. Defining conflict: Trends, levels and type of conflicts

Conflict does not necessarily have to be expressed through violent struggle, nor is the outcome of conflict always detrimental to long-term development. For example, conflict can be expressed through organized protests, which may result in the resolution of grievances. At times conflicts can also result in an upheaval of societal structures and a reorganization based on more meritocratic and equitable principles. However, the combination of direct humanitarian and physical costs and the indirect psychological scars make violent conflict particularly undesirable. Thus, less disruptive approaches to resolution exist and are preferable.

The Uppsala Conflict Data Program (UCDP) framework defines conflict as *"a contested incompatibility that concerns government and/or territory where the use of armed force between two parties, of which at least one is the Government of a State, results in at least 25 battle-related deaths in a calendar year."*[6] There are some limitations of adopting this definition, which include, for example, the fact that it ignores conflict that involves few or no casualties, but which can be protracted and equally, if not more detrimental to development. Nevertheless, doing so provides a baseline for comparison across countries against which to measure conflict.

Analysis of the drivers of conflict requires understanding the evolution of conflict and distinctions in the types of conflict, where one can distinguish between 'external' and 'internal' conflicts (Ghani and Iyer, 2010). The former involves a clash between two different States (interstate war) and the latter refers to a clush within the borders of a State (intrastate conflict or civil war) and can occur at the subnational or community level and can involve clashes between communities or armed groups.

A distinction can also be made based upon whether the parties involved are State-based or non-State groups. State-based conflict takes place between non-State actors (such as separatist or terrorist groups) and the State, while conflicts between non-governmental groups that usually manifest at the subnational level tend to occur between culturally formed groups within a society such as ethnic, religious and regional groups.

Most conflicts today take the form of intrastate or civil conflicts (the light green area of figure 1.2). The major interstate wars that ravaged previous decades were also contestations between the most advanced nations economically and militarily. The conflicts of the twenty-first century are of a different mould, as the drivers are more socio-economically oriented and the States involved are typically mired in low levels of development.

Many internal armed conflicts are also taking on an international dimension ("internationalized intrastate conflict" accounting for 18 out of 51 armed conflicts in 2016, as illustrated by the blue area of figure 1.2). Although external involvement in intrastate conflicts has been a phenomenon since the 1960s, the increase since 2012 has been unprecedented. Unfortunately, the availability of external support makes these conflicts particularly protracted and lethal (Melander and others, 2016).

The shift in the type of conflict since the Second World War from predominantly interstate confrontations to primarily intrastate clashes suggests that conflict today is driven by increasing discontent due to structural socio-economic and institutional conditions within societies, rather than geopolitically motivated provocations from external actors. Thus, the prevention of conflicts in the twenty-first century is increasingly dependent on

Figure 1.2. State-based armed conflicts (by type of conflict) that have taken place globally, 1946-2016

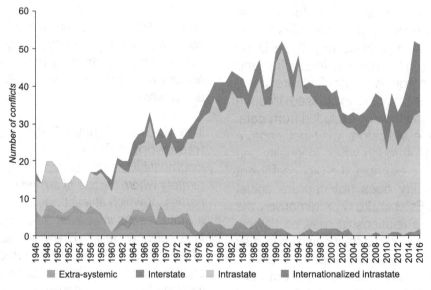

Source: ESCAP, based on data from the Uppsala Conflict Data Programme. Accessed 8 February 2018.

Note: State-based armed conflicts refer to those with a minimum of 25 battle-related deaths in one calendar year and in which at least one actor is the Government of a State. "Internationalized intrastate" conflicts are a type of intrastate conflict in which one or more outside States support one of the warring parties. An "extra-systemic" conflicts refers to a conflict between a State and a non-State group outside the State.

the ability of home Governments to foster the type of balanced development that can spur an upward spiral of mutually reinforcing peace and development outcomes.

Another defining feature of modern conflicts is worth highlighting. Unlike earlier revolutions of the twentieth century that were primarily driven by the "Marxian" type of economic class struggle, today's conflicts are increasingly based on ethnic, religious or regional cleavages (Ray and Esteban, 2017). This evolution was most eloquently captured by Horowitz (1985), who remarked that *"in much of Asia and Africa, it is only modest hyperbole to assert that the Marxian prophecy has had an ethnic fulfillment."* Ethnic conflict in particular can create deep fissures that are difficult to resolve, as the underlying tensions are driven by intrinsic motivations related to identity. Conceptual frameworks distinguish between primordialism and instrumentalism in diagnosing ethnic conflicts. The former refers to an inherent tendency of hatred towards other groups and thus an inevitable "Huntington" clash of civilizations that can be resolved by independence or some form of self-determination (Huntington, 1993). The latter is more nuanced and suggests that ethnicity can be exploited to mobilize group support for apparent or underlying economic or political motives. The latter set of risks could possibly be alleviated by addressing socio-economic concerns and enshrining "institutionalized equality" for all groups.

The Asia-Pacific region is home to some of the most intense contestations between ethnic and/or religious groups such as in Bangladesh and Myanmar; at the same time, the region is also home to prosperous, ethnically diverse societies such as Singapore and Malaysia. Thus, conflict is not always an inevitability of diversity. Understanding how markers such as ethnicity can be used to organize similar individuals along opposing lines will require a survey of the multidimensional impacts and causes of conflict.

2. Multidimensional impacts and causes

Abstracting from complex historical and political underpinnings of conflict, one can trace mutually reinforcing links between peace and sustainable development. For example, stable and conducive societies tend to attract more capital, particularly longer-term investment, thereby creating jobs and allowing for long-term productivity growth. In such economies, the opportunity cost of conflict tends to be higher. Similarly, improved social outcomes (such as greater education attainment, better health and more poverty alleviation, and provision of basic services) also mitigate the risks of conflict through multiple channels. For example, besides augmenting human capital, and thereby targeting structural drivers of conflict, education in conflict-affected situations can also serve as a means of socialization and identity development by transmitting knowledge, skills, values and attitudes across generations (Smith, 2010). Environmental development in the form of inclusive access policies, disaster preparedness and conservation efforts can also minimize the risks of conflict by ensuring fairness, sustainability and resilience. When such outcomes are achieved, countries can witness an upward spiral of peace and sustainable development.

Conversely, conflict can unravel development gains by destroying physical capital and infrastructure, thereby impeding economic activity and raising transaction costs. For example, declining economic activity and informalization of employment narrows the taxable base (Looney, 2006). This can lead to deterioration in fiscal positions as well as lower investment in socio-economic development in conflict afflicted countries, particularly given the increasing share of public expenditure that is diverted towards defence and security purposes in such an environment. In addition, the likelihood of marginalization in fragile settings is higher; and the consequent rise in socio-economic vulnerabilities may increase the propensity for civilians to engage in further conflict. Moreover, providing relief to those affected by natural disasters and ensuring adequate environmental conservation is more difficult in countries that are engaged in conflict. This increases levels of vulnerability in affected populations further, fuelling tensions and conflict.

Given this mutually reinforcing and inter dependent relationship, it must be underscored that a compartmentalized approach that fails to integrate the three dimensions of sustainable development will not be sufficient to secure peace and prevent conflict. Furthermore, development must go beyond aggregate outcomes and encompass intrinsic notions of well-being such as human rights, security and "institutionalized respect" for diversity, as growth on its own does not necessarily translate into more peaceful conditions. This is particularly the case when the benefits of development are shared unevenly within society. For example, despite registering some of the highest growth rates in the world, Myanmar has experienced bouts of civil conflict. Unsuspectingly, economic development through rapid, unregulated market liberalization has, at times, resulted in political instability. For example, dramatic capital account liberalization exploited by crony capitalism in some South-East and East Asian countries in the early 1990s led to a real estate bubble, the bursting of which eventually resulted in economic, political and social turmoil. On the political front, the assumption of "democratic peace" and reforms towards democratization has not panned out as expected, resulting instead in increased violence due to historic path-dependence (Reilly, 2002).

Clearly, an upward spiral of durable peace and sustainable development is not a foregone conclusion, and significant heterogeneity exists even among the group of countries either experiencing conflict or in fragile situations. In some contexts, the driving forces are social whereas in others they are economic. In some contexts, the dividing lines are ideological whereas in others they are ethnic or religious. Nevertheless, a recurring theme that can be gleaned from all cases is that all these countries suffer from some form of institutional shortcomings such as low levels of resilience or capacities to deal with shocks.

Given the multidimensionality of peace and development, a holistic assessment that considers interrelated spheres such as the political economy, social construct and institutional set-up is critical. Accordingly, many organizations have undergone a fundamental shift towards frameworks that are more comprehensive than the narrow categorization of fragility, with revised models that capture the diversity of risks as well as vulnerabilities that induce fragility. Capturing the multidimensionality of the phenomenon in terms of impacts is also necessary. The significant spillovers and interconnectedness of seemingly disparate elements during conflicts also warrants a more integrated framework of analysis. The impacts of conflicts are cross-cutting, manifesting directly in the form of battle-related fatalities and destruction of property; the secondary impacts of conflict unfold gradually in the form of indirect deaths or reduced potential output as a result of the direct impacts. In fact, the severe destruction of infrastructure could, in the long term, induce as many indirect deaths, since health care depends highly on a good infrastructure and smoothly running supply chains (Chen and others, 2008).

Finally, multidimensionality and quantitative delineations must be complemented by a comprehension of the more qualitative historical, political and socio-cultural context within which the causes or so-called "risk factors" translate into actual conflict. A more complete assessment of recent civil wars in the Asia-Pacific region suggests that a confluence of conditions eventually led to violence. These include a weakening of the democratic State, the development of a dissident organization and its role in serving as a unifying voice, particularly in rural parts of the region. This resonates with the widely understood sequential tracing of the process through which political violence manifests, beginning with the development of discontent, politicization of discontent, to its actualization in the form of political violence (Gurr, 1971).

Considering the complexity of the subject, it is crucial for this report to be consistent in the understanding and the measurement of peace and conflict. While box 1.1 outlines some of the existing indices of conflict and security that vary in terms of their coverage across countries and time frame, this report henceforth relies mainly on INFORM, which is a global tool designed to understand the risk of humanitarian crises. Developed by the Inter-Agency Standing Committee[7] Task Team for Preparedness and Resilience Capacities of the United Nations and non-United Nations humanitarian partners, the framework consists of 53 core indicators intended to measure the following three dimensions of risk: (a) the exposure to natural and human-made hazards; (b) the socio-economic vulnerability and the susceptibility of communities to those hazards; and (c) institutional and infrastructure capacities to address disasters and violent conflicts (table 1.1).[8]

Coverage of issues, country-coverage and timespan is most comprehensive for INFORM, thereby justifying its use. As highlighted above, a distinction between the "absence of conflict" and "durable peace" is essential, since the former does not necessarily imply that a society is "risk-

free". Conflict is an inherently latent phenomenon influenced by multidimensional factors, that once triggered can escalate to destabilizing levels. Thus, it is critical to capture the underlying structural drivers of conflict even in the absence of conflict. The comprehensiveness of INFORM dimensionally, complemented by its granularity across variables, makes it a powerful framework for assessing the building blocks of conflict prevention and durable peace. In addition to countries where civil conflict is unfolding, INFORM draws attention to contexts where the structural factors of conflict are also evident. The conceptual overlaps between the SDGs and INFORM also lend further analytical convenience.

Box 1.1. Indices of conflict and security

A growing stratum of the literature has been devoted to developing methodologies to identify and quantitatively measure risks of conflict. The Index for Risk Management (INFORM), the OECD States of Fragility Index, the Fragile States Index (FSI) of the Fund for Peace, and the World Bank's Political Stability and Absence of Violence Index are some of the indices to which reference is frequently made. They assign weights to various dimensions of peace based on the mandates of respective efforts.

INFORM measures the risk of humanitarian crises and disasters occurring by tracking the three conceptual dimensions of risk-exposure, vulnerability and coping capacity. This effectively suggests a holistic approach to "sustaining peace" by emphasizing risk prevention, preparedness and responses. In contrast, the FSI measures a narrower outcome such as the vulnerability of a State to experiencing collapse or conflict. The Political Stability and Absence of Violence Index measures the likelihood of violence, terrorism or instability in a country from the political perspective. The Global Peace Index is a quantification of the state of negative peace[a] of a nation through three main areas – the ongoing domestic and international peacefulness, the level of national cohesion and a country's militarization. The State Fragility Index assesses the effectiveness and legitimacy of countries in four performance dimensions – economic, security, social and political. The Political Instability Index provides a quantification of social, political and economic drivers of political instability based on two dimensions – vulnerability and economic distress.

Most indices increasingly attempt to capture the interconnected and multifaced elements of conflict (table A) transcending the usual description of conflicts that are narrowly focused on the immediate context. These indices can conceptually be bifurcated into two domains - an exposure component and a resilience component. The exposure component normally attempts to capture some underlying structural elements such as susceptibility to disasters, socio-economic vulnerability and the inclusiveness of development outcomes. High disparities in the distribution of development benefits will naturally increase the level of exposure to conflict. Alternatively, the resilience component captures the capacity – institutional or infrastructure – of countries to absorb shocks such as natural disasters, economic turbulence or other triggers. It is the interaction between these two components that determines a country's risk level.

[a] Negative peace is defined as the absence of violence. The term "negative" implies that violence can erupt anytime. An example of this is a ceasefire. This concept is different from positive peace, which refers to the overall conditions leading to stability, including justice, equality, enforcement of law, etc. (Galtung, 1996).

Box 1.1. *(continued)*

Table A. Summary of various indices

Index	Coverage of countries with special needs (Out of 29 regional member States of ESCAP)	Time span	Source	Social	Economic	Political	Peace and Security	Internal	External	Natural
States of Fragility	22	2005-2016 (12 years)	Organisation for Economic Co-operation and Development (OECD)	√	√	√	√	√	√	√
Fragile State Index	22	2006-2017 (12 years)	Fund for Peace	√	√	√	√	√	√	
State Fragility Index	19	1995-2016 (22 years)	Centre for Systemic Peace	√	√	√	√	√		
Global Peace Index	17	2008-2017 (10 years)	Institute for Economics and Peace	√		√	√	√	√	
Political Instability Index	17	2007; 2009/2010 (2 years)	Economic Intelligence Unit	√	√	√	√	√	√	
Political Stability and Absence of Violence	29	1996-2015 (19 years)	World Bank	√		√	√	√	√	
Index for Risk Management (INFORM)	29	2012-2018 (7 years)	Inter-Agency Standing Committee and the European Commission	√	√	√	√	√		√

Source: ESCAP.

Table 1.1. Dimensions and components of INFORM

Ranking level	INFORM																
Concept level (Dimensions)	Hazard and exposure							Vulnerability					Lack of coping capacity				
Functional level (Categories)	Natural					Human		Socio-economic			Vulnerable groups		Institutional		Infrastructure		
Component level	Earthquake	Tsunami	Flood	Tropical cyclone	Drought	Current conflict intensity	Projected conflict risk	Development & Deprivation (50%)	Inequality (25%)	Aid dependency (25%)	Uprooted people	Other vulnerable groups	Disaster risk reduction	Governance	Communication	Physical infrastructure	Access to health system

Source: Inter-Agency Standing Committee and the European Commission.

Importantly, the indices are highly correlated with each other (figure 1.3), although there may also be pronounced distinctions for countries that have recently experienced humanitarian crises or disasters but whose risks of future crisis are lower than their historical norm. For example, while a previously civil war-ravaged Timor-Leste is identified as a fragile State with an "alert level" of fragility according to FSI, the risk of crises and disasters is considered "medium" by INFORM, supported by its low level of human hazard and exposure.[9] Similarly, Uzbekistan is at a "high warning level" of fragility by FSI, but the risk of humanitarian crises is "low" because it is one of the best performing countries among the Asia-Pacific countries with special needs in terms of coping with the susceptibility of its communities to hazards.

C. 2030 Agenda, peace and security

The SDGs seek to address some of the shortcomings of the Millennium Development Goals (MDGs) by integrating the three dimensions of development and the requisite implementation modalities at the national and international levels. While the pursuit of the MDGs has been hampered by "conflict, a lack of rule of law and weak institutions" (UNDP, 2016b), the 2030 Agenda offers a more robust and integrated framework for development.

A high degree of association between the capacity of countries to pursue the SDGs and their risk levels can be observed (figure 1.4), with countries that have very low levels of risk demonstrating a much higher capacity for attaining sustainable development than those at a high level of risk. This is to be expected as the priorities identified in the SDGs are in strong alignment with the dimensions necessary for fostering peace. Harnessing the synergies and complementarities across the 17 SDGs can also contribute to the type of holistic development that nudge nations into an upward spiral of peace and development.

The all-encompassing nature of the SDGs suggests that such a pursuit could genuinely foster the type of mutually reinforcing peace and development outcomes discussed above. A quick glance at the dimensions of peace and conflict indices such as INFORM and the SDGs suggests a high degree of overlapping priorities. It can be seen that the components of INFORM resonate with almost every sustainable development goal.[10]

Figure 1.3. Index for Risk Management and Fragile States Index

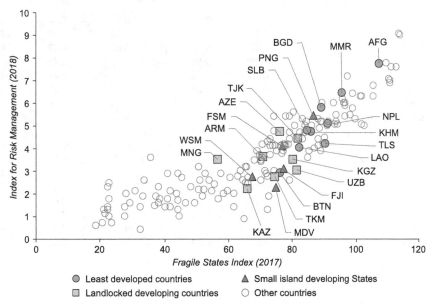

Source: ESCAP, based on the Fragile States Index for 2017 from the Fund for Peace and the INFORM for 2018 from the Inter-Agency Standing Committee and the European Commission. Accessed 20 November 2017.
Note: Country names and codes are available in the explanatory notes.

Figure 1.4. SDGs capacities and conflict risk and fragility

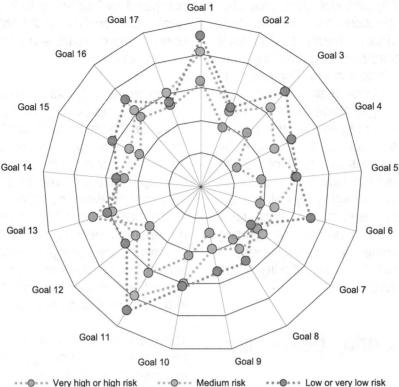

· · ◉ · · Very high or high risk   · · ◉ · · Medium risk   · · ◉ · · Low or very low risk

Source: ESCAP, based on data from Cho and others (2016), ESCAP (2016) and the Inter-Agency Standing Committee and the European Commission. Accessed 20 November 2017.

Note: The closer that a country group is to centre of the graph, the lower the SDGs capacity.

Table 1.2. Mapping SDGs and INFORM dimensions

SDGs	INFORM Natural	Human	Socio-economic vulnerability	Vulnerable groups	Institutional	Infrastructure
1 No poverty	0.07	-0.32	-0.81	-0.44	-0.47	-0.83
2 Zero hunger	-0.27	-0.24	-0.40	-0.33	-0.27	-0.38
3 Good health and well-being	-0.05	-0.50	-0.81	-0.52	-0.64	-0.92
4 Quality education	-0.19	-0.54	-0.78	-0.46	-0.67	-0.82
5 Gender equality	-0.13	-0.51	-0.72	-0.45	-0.68	-0.68
6 Clean water & sanitation	-0.24	-0.55	-0.80	-0.51	-0.67	-0.91
7 Affordable and clean energy	0.08	0.02	-0.05	0.00	-0.05	0.05
8 Decent work and economic growth	-0.12	-0.49	-0.70	-0.39	-0.81	-0.70
9 Industry, innovation and infrastructure	-0.12	-0.47	-0.81	-0.44	-0.81	-0.86
10 Reduced inequalities	-0.15	-0.32	-0.68	-0.33	-0.51	-0.70
11 Sustainable cities, and communities	0.02	-0.44	-0.82	-0.52	-0.58	-0.91
12 Responsible consumption and production	-0.11	-0.47	-0.14	-0.26	-0.34	-0.23
13 Climate action	-0.12	0.18	0.43	0.25	0.19	0.40
14 Life below water	-0.24	-0.04	0.29	0.03	0.32	0.32
15 Life on land	-0.51	-0.49	-0.36	-0.39	-0.36	-0.50
16 Peace, justice and strong institutions	-0.02	-0.40	-0.57	-0.43	-0.61	-0.55
17 Partnerships for the Goals	0.02	-0.24	-0.62	-0.10	-0.65	-0.56

High -   Low   High +

-1   0   1

Source: ESCAP, based on data from Cho and others (2016), ESCAP (2016) and the Inter-Agency Standing Committee and the European Commission. Accessed 20 November 2017.

Note: The values refer to Pearson's correlation coefficients. The exercise covers a set of 175 countries for which the latest data are available.

A statistical mapping exercise corroborates the fact that there is a high degree of alignment between the SDGs and measures of conflict (table 1.2). In essence there is a predominantly inverse correlation between the parameters that capture risk levels and the progress (or lack of) in reaching the SDGs, with the correlation ranging from -0.92 to 0.43. It can be seen that the negative correlation between the two are particularly strong across the INFORM dimensions of socio-economic vulnerability, institutional and infrastructure coping capacity. For example, the correlation between the infrastructure domain and Goal 6 on "good health and well-being" is significant at -0.92. This is consistent with findings that successful health-care delivery heavily depends on reliable infrastructure and smooth supply chains, and how the destruction of conflict can impede outcomes as highlighted above (Chen and others, 2008).

D. Conclusion

The nexus between sustainable development and sustaining peace is multidimensional, exhibiting significant spillovers thereby requiring an integrated approach for peace-building. Globally, a fundamental shift has taken place in recent decades from primarily interstate to intrastate confrontations. In the twenty-first century, peace and stability is therefore increasingly dependent on the ability of national Governments and the international community to foster development that nudges societies into an upward spiral of mutually reinforcing peace and development outcomes.

Clarifying the distinction between the "absence of conflict" and "durable peace", this chapter has argued that the absence of conflict does not fulfill the conditions of durable peace. As an inherently latent phenomenon, the risks of conflict depend upon structural factors that can be triggered under various conditions. These underlying risk factors, such as poverty, inequality and natural resource dependence, are particularly pronounced in countries with special needs, as demonstrated in chapter 3. Given the latency of conflict, even peaceful conditions can escalate to destabilizing levels quite swiftly. Thus, a dynamic and holistic assessment of a country's susceptibility to conflict is necessary.

ENDNOTES

1 See http://www.undp.org/content/undp/en/home/sustainable-development-goals/goal-16-peace-justice-and-strong-institutions.html.

2 A/RES/70/262, preamble.

3 The Institute for Economics and Peace imputes the total cost based on items such as military expenditure, GDP losses from conflict, cost of security, losses due to violent crime, homicide, incarceration and terrorism as well as United Nations peacekeeping expenditure.

4 A/RES/70/262, para. 35.

5 Ray and Esteban (2017) allude to the presence of threshold effects. While the drivers of conflict may be active at all economic levels, poverty allows that conflict to fully express itself.

6 UCDP/PRIO Armed Conflict Dataset Codebook1.

7 See endnote 7 of Introduction.

8 The components of each dimension are aggregated to a value ranging from zero to 10, with higher values indicating higher risk. The composite INFORM figure is then acquired using a geometric average of the three dimensions. The countries are then separated into five risk groups according to their performance in every dimension: "very high"; "high"; "medium"; "low"; and "very low". The threshold level for each dimension is available in the Annex.

9 Risk levels of Asia-Pacific least developed countries, landlocked developing countries and small island developing States and corresponding scores are available in the Annex.

10 Similarly, the OECD States of Fragility Index, which captures fragility across five clusters that include economic foundations, justice, violence, institutions and resilience, also concurs with the tenets of the SDGs.

CHAPTER 2

The landscape of conflict in Asia and the Pacific

The Asia-Pacific region is diverse across multiple dimensions – geographically, from the steppes of Central Asia to the tropics of South-East Asia and the Pacific island countries, and economically, from the advanced status of countries such as Australia and Japan to those embroiled in civil conflict and trapped in least developed country status such as Afghanistan. While the region has exhibited stellar development performance, it has witnessed nearly the same level of armed conflict as Africa which has invariably hampered progress (figure 2.1).

For example, Cambodia, which is a post-conflict least developed country, witnessed stagnant and even regressing Human Assets Index (HAI)[1] outcomes during its civil war, with measurements improving steadily after restoration of political stability following the general elections in 1998 (Kim and Sauter, 2017).[2] War torn Afghanistan currently reports the lowest HAI scores in Asia-Pacific and one of the lowest in the world, although there has been noteworthy progress primarily due to significant levels of ODA channelled to the social sectors. In Nepal, the decade-long internal armed conflict that had a significant rural dimension impeded rural development outcomes. Prolonged internal conflict in Myanmar has created parallel subnational administrations run by ethnic armed organizations, thereby impeding development as well as broader political and social reforms (The Asia Foundation, 2017).

Since the impacts of conflict translate through various channels, some regional peculiarities are worth underscoring. Despite the prevalence of conflicts, the resilience of income growth – albeit modest – in Asia and the Pacific diverges from the experience of other regions such as sub-Saharan Africa where the trajectory has been particularly volatile (figure 2.2). The experience of Sri Lanka (although not a country with special needs) – a nation beleaguered by a conflict for 26 years, while registering steady increases in per capita income – demonstrates that growth can continue even in the time of civil war. This may be due to the largely geographic concentration of the conflict in the northern and eastern parts of the country, regions that are isolated from the rest of the formal economy.

Figure 2.1. State-based armed conflict by region, 1946-2016

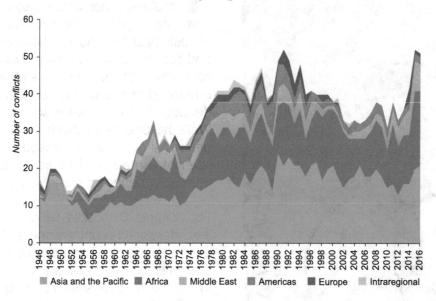

Source: ESCAP, based on data from the Uppsala Conflict Data Programme. Accessed 8 February 2018.

Note: State-based armed conflicts refer to those with a minimum of 25 battle-related deaths in one calendar year and in which at least one actor is the Government of a state.

Figure 2.2. Evolution of GDP per capita in conflict-affected countries of the Asia-Pacific and sub-Saharan Africa regions, 1970-2016

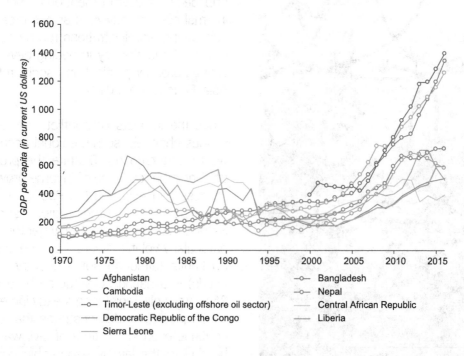

Source: ESCAP, based on data from the National Account Main Aggregates Database, United Nations Department of Economic and Social Affairs, and the World Bank national accounts data. Accessed 21 March 2018.

Note: Data are reported in current United States dollars. Asia-Pacific least developed countries that have experienced or are experiencing some form of conflict are denoted by the circle markers.

Similarly, Nepal also registered decent growth despite the simmering tensions that preceded the insurgency as well as during the war. This again was perhaps due to the largely rural concentration of the conflict. Alternatively, it could be due to differences in dependence on natural resource commodities, as the lack of diversification in economies of sub-Saharan Africa increases their exposure to negative impacts of conflict. Neighbourhood effects may also play an explanatory role, as many conflict-affected countries in sub-Saharan Africa are also surrounded by other conflict countries, which was not the case in the Asia-Pacific region.

What makes the Asia-Pacific region's conflicts particularly destructive is the protracted nature of the disputes, with subnational conflicts lasting on average 45.2 years in South and South-East Asia, more than twice the global average of 16.8 years (The Asia Foundation, 2017).

The INFORM identifies 11 "very high" and "high" risk countries in the Asia-Pacific region, including five countries with special needs: Afghanistan, Bangladesh, Myanmar, Nepal and Papua New Guinea (figure 2.3). Across the three groups of

countries with special needs, least developed countries on average record the highest risk levels. However, the INFORM risk classification appears to be only weakly correlated with least developed country status, with only one in three least developed countries classified as a "very high" or "high" risk, whereas 6 out of 16 other developing countries in the region belong to these categories. As for landlocked or small island developing States, 11 out of 14 are "low" or "very low" risk countries. On average, these countries are not riskier than the average Asia-Pacific developing country; this can be ascribed to the very low "human hazard" risk in small island developing States and low "socio-economic vulnerability" in the case of landlocked developing countries (figure 2.4).

Across the Asia-Pacific region, risk levels and their drivers vary considerably. From the currently low-risk Central Asian landlocked developing countries (of which some have seen increased activities by extremist groups) to the relatively high-risk least developed countries in South Asia, a dynamic and contextual assessment of the landscape is necessary. The inherent latency of conflict also suggests that a static view of the context is

Figure 2.3. INFORM scores for Asia-Pacific countries with special needs, 2018

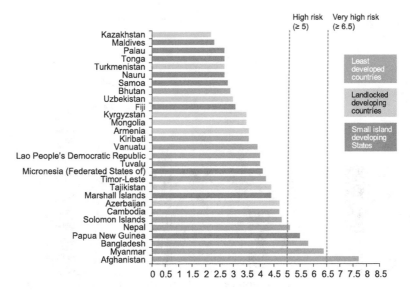

Source: Inter-Agency Standing Committee and the European Commission. Accessed 20 November 2017.

Note: See endnote 7 of Introduction.

not adequate as a singular event, if unresolved, can also have destabilizing consequences. For example, although a few countries are ranked by INFORM as low risk, current domestic instability and transboundary tensions could suggest a different risk classification despite strong underlying socio-economic fundamentals. Given the structural vulnerabilities of these economies, even small changes in the status quo could thwart development progress.

The diversity in the region is further substantiated by the widely varying risk profiles displayed by countries with special needs and other developing countries at the disaggregated level of INFORM (figure 2.4). While least developed countries exhibit the highest levels of vulnerability, they lack coping capacity, which exacerbates their situation. Landlocked developing countries, small island developing States and other Asia-Pacific developing countries show similar scores on average, despite their risks being driven by different factors:

(a) Other Asia-Pacific developing countries are exposed to the highest level of hazard and exposure, while having the strongest coping capacity;

(b) The risk level of small island developing States is underestimated by INFORM – which does not include climate factors – but are still second to least developed countries in terms of vulnerability and the lack of coping capacity; and

(c) Landlocked developing countries have a relatively high level of hazard and a weak coping capacity.

Although the risk levels of countries with special needs have generally been trending downwards in recent years, the latency of conflict and the risk of escalation to destabilizing levels once a conflict is triggered warrants continued surveillance of the underlying drivers.

Figure 2.5 shows that natural hazards are more consequential than human conflicts when assessing risk levels in the Asia-Pacific region. In terms of vulnerability, the risks of least developed countries and small island developing States are mostly driven by their socio-economic vulnerability, such as high levels of poverty, inequality and dependency on external aid. Finally, the weak coping capacity of least developed countries stems both from their institutional and from infrastructure deficits.

Figure 2.4. INFORM and its three dimensions, by country group, 2018

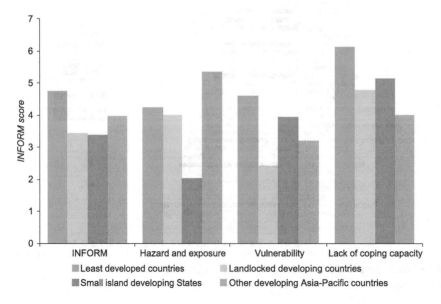

Source: ESCAP, based on data from the Inter-Agency Standing Committee and the European Commission. Accessed 20 November 2017.

Figure 2.5. INFORM and its six categories, by country group, 2018

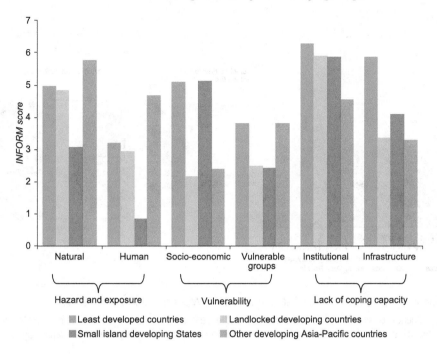

Source: ESCAP, based on data from the Inter-Agency Standing Committee and the European Commission. Accessed 20 November 2017.

A. Conflict in countries with special needs

Asia-Pacific countries with special needs are, or have been, the locus of some of the most egregious and destructive conflicts in human history – from the abating but ongoing conflict in Afghanistan that has claimed around 181,000 lives, to the Khmer regime in Cambodia that resulted in the genocide of more than 2 million people. On the surface, the death toll may not appear alarming when compared to other fatalities such as the millions that perish in traffic accidents or those that succumb to deadly diseases. However, the impacts of such deaths are broader than numbers, as the spectre of conflict casualties causes affected locations to deteriorate into insecure settings that breed psychological trauma, social discord and a collapse of the "rule of law" – all outcomes that are inimical to development (UNDP, 2008).

Countries with special needs are confronted by significant structural impediments to development, and consequently exhibit a high level of vulnerability

to shocks that are either socio-economic or environmental in nature. Moreover, given their resource constraints, they also possess limited capacities to cope with such shocks, making them more susceptible to conflicts. Least developed countries are characterized by lower levels of socio-economic development and economic vulnerabilities, whereas small island developing States face the constant risk of rising sea-levels and tropical storms. The eruption of conflict in such contexts can exacerbate the already formidable structural impediments to development. For example, when Nepal was reeling from the devastation of the earthquake in 2015, it was hit by a contestation over a proposed constitutional revision. As a landlocked country heavily dependent on imports from India, the conflict involved a border blockade, which was particularly damaging, with inflation reaching double digits.

In terms of fatalities, it should be noted that while the number of conflicts where at least 25 persons were killed is higher in other developing countries, the total death toll is higher in least developed countries (figure 2.6, panel A). Again, the results here are driven by a group of countries,

Figure 2.6. Conflicts and fatalities in Asia and the Pacific

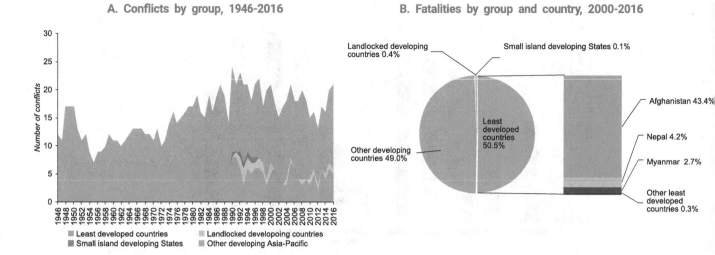

A. Conflicts by group, 1946-2016

B. Fatalities by group and country, 2000-2016

Source: ESCAP, based on data from the Uppsala Conflict Data Program, 2016. Accessed 10 November 2017.

Note: Panel A portrays the incidence of conflicts where at least 25 battle deaths were reported. Panel B reflects the share of battle deaths by country group in the region's total between 2000 and 2016, while displaying the major countries separately.

i.e., Afghanistan, Myanmar and Nepal for least developed countries and other developing countries (figure 2.6, panel B). This asymmetry suggests that conflicts are more intense in countries with special needs but more widespread in other developing countries. Second, the State's ability to decisively bring closure to a conflict is perhaps a determining factor. In Afghanistan and Myanmar, significant tracts of territory are beyond the remit of the State and instead are governed by armed groups that form a parallel administration.

The profiles of conflict across countries in the region is also fairly heterogenous. For example, in Afghanistan state-based conflict has predominated, whereas in Myanmar until recently one-sided conflicts were more widespread but have been overtaken by state-based clashes. Although violent conflict is less frequent in Bangladesh, political turmoil continues to hamper national solidarity, whereas separatism and the drive towards autonomy has fuelled tensions in Myanmar and Nepal (The Asia Foundation 2017). The landscape in Myanmar is also characterized by large-scale communal and ideological conflicts. Local conflicts over resources and community rights are also prevalent in Cambodia, Myanmar

and Nepal, whereas in Mongolia urban crime and violence are the more prevalent forms of tension (The Asia Foundation, 2017). In the low-lying atoll countries of the Pacific, sea-level rise, saltwater intrusion, floods and prolonged droughts are already having severe impacts on the limited and fragile freshwater supplies, which could lead to social tensions as climate change worsens.

In addition to the economic costs and fatalities, the provision of humanitarian assistance in the face of a conflict is also particularly challenging, given geographic and infrastructure constraints. Thus, an understanding of the dimensions that make countries with special needs more susceptible to conflicts is critical to ensuring that the global programmes of action for this group of countries can be implemented without the risk of backtracking. A deeper understanding must first explain the forces behind the general rise in intrastate conflicts.

1. Why is there a rise in intrastate conflicts?

Given their domestic structural vulnerabilities, countries with special needs are more susceptible to intrastate conflict. A more politico-historical narrative suggests that this could be due to either (or both) of the following: first, the inheritance of colonial era institutional structures meant that associated governance practices and rules of engagement were not natively conceived to ensure an alignment of social and private objectives. Second, a more sociological explanation criticizes the post-colonial territorial arrangements that were not sensitive to ethnic distribution and resulted in the amalgamation of multiple ethnic groups that had no common history of state-building and are now engaged in a struggle for self-determination. Indeed, it has been argued that some of these States are a product of colonialism and a historical accident rather than having resulted naturally (Reilly, 2002). This is evident in Papua New Guinea and the Solomon Islands where *"small stateless traditional societies were aggregated for the purposes of international statehood into weak and impoverished modern States, some of which lack the capacity to fulfil such fundamental state tasks as tax collection or delivery of basic services"* (Reilly, 2002). This history may have contributed to making them more vulnerable, socio-economically.

A related issue is the incomplete democratization of many of these countries. While normative inclinations may dictate that long-term democracies are, on average, less susceptible to internal conflict, the process of democratization itself can be turbulent (Mansfield and Snyder, 1995). For example, in ethnically diverse States, rapid democratization could result in ethnically based self-determination and secessionist movements (De Nevers, 1993).

The landscape of conflict in Asia and the Pacific, which depicts a growing incidence of conflicts in countries with special needs marked by an increasingly internal orientation of incidences, can be organized into two layers of inquiries. First, why are countries with special needs more prone to conflict? Second, why are intrastate conflicts more prevalent? Thus, while the more global trend of a precipitous decline in interstate conflicts is perhaps due to the evolving architecture and effectiveness of multilateralism, its replacement by internally driven conflicts in countries with special needs may be due to internal socio-economic vulnerabilities and weak coping capacities. It can

be argued that the current international architecture for dispute resolution acknowledges the State as the basic unit of international order, but such approaches are not easy to deploy for intrastate conflicts as the primacy of state sovereignty tends to militate against timely intervention. Moreover, while the end of the cold war was pivotal in defusing earlier stalemates, thereby increasing international cooperation and decreasing the incidence of interstate wars, intrastate conflicts are now a greater threat to peace than major interstate confrontations (Yilmaz, 2007).

Another complicating factor is that intrastate conflicts are rarely a continuous phenomenon and instead exhibit a cyclicality that swings between low- and high-intensity warfare with the low-intensity stages lasting far longer (UNDP, 2008). This implies that such conflicts are protracted and particularly challenging to resolve. For countries with special needs the secular ramifications of protracted conflicts are grave and compound their structural weaknesses. Thus, a related discussion is whether conflict should be an additional criterion in determining least developed country status, considering the fact that two-thirds of the least developed countries are trapped in conflict (Kim and Sauter, 2017). The abundance of fragile countries in the least developed country grouping also lends credence to the story that the structural fault lines and associated adverse development outcomes are attributable to the vacuum left by colonialism.

2. How do risk levels vary across the Asia-Pacific countries with special needs?

Mainstream analyses of conflict or potential conflict in Asia and the Pacific focus primarily on the geo-political struggle for regional hegemony among the more powerful States (Swaine and others, 2015). However, several countries with special needs have, in recent years, experienced or continue to experience violent conflict in one form or the other. Yet, as noted above, not all countries with special needs exhibit high-risk levels. Thus, whereas INFORM identifies Afghanistan as being at a very high-risk level and Bangladesh, Myanmar and Papua New Guinea as high-risk, Bhutan, Kazakhstan and Turkmenistan – each also a country with special needs – are considered as low risk. The complexities associated with assessing risk levels and their contributing factors become more evident when considering the socio-economically more developed and low-risk Central Asian countries that are recording an increasing number of combatants fighting for extremist groups. A related and longer-term implication is the prospect of these combatants returning home and fuelling radicalism further.

While Asia-Pacific countries with special needs continue to grapple with development challenges, risk levels have generally been trending downwards in recent years. Most countries with special needs are clustered around low and medium levels of risk and have not demonstrated significant movements (figure 2.7).

Kyrgyzstan has exhibited the highest decrease in risk levels in recent years from high risk to medium risk (and at one point even low risk). This was primarily driven by a precipitous decline in the risk of 'human hazard' and 'vulnerable groups'. Risk levels also declined significantly in the Lao

People's Democratic Republic, which also switched from being a high-risk country to a medium risk country in response to improvements that have taken place across the various dimensions of risk, especially in the area of "human hazards". Conversely, Marshall Islands and Tuvalu have recorded the highest increases in risk levels, primarily due to increases in the risks of hazards and socio-economic vulnerability.

Importantly, higher-risk countries such as Afghanistan, Myanmar and Nepal have exhibited a downward trend. In Afghanistan, the gradual decrease is attributable to marginal improvements in coping capacities, although underlying factors such as the number of vulnerable groups and uprooted people have been increasing. In Myanmar, risk levels have been buttressed by improvements in infrastructure and communications; however, further progress is being obstructed by a deterioration in the plight of vulnerable groups. In Nepal, gradual and consistent declines can be observed evenly across the dimensions of coping capacity and socio-economic vulnerability.

Figure 2.7. INFORM status and six-year trends

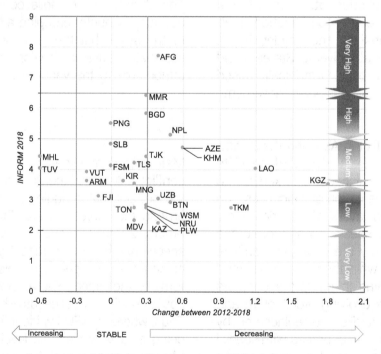

Source: ESCAP, based on data from the Inter-Agency Standing Committee and the European Commissions. Accessed 20 November 2017.
Note: Country names and codes are available in the explanatory notes.

B. Conclusion

Countries with special needs are confronted with significant structural impediments that have trapped them in low levels of development. Such outcomes also translate into higher risks of conflict through increased socio-economic vulnerabilities as well as limited institutional and infrastructure capacities to deal with shocks. An outbreak of conflict in such contexts can compound the pre-existing conditions.

While their vulnerabilities suggest that countries with special needs should theoretically be more susceptible to conflicts, this report's assessment reveals a very heterogenous spectrum of risk profiles in the Asia-Pacific region. Indeed five of the 11 high-risk countries in the region are countries with special needs. When decomposing INFORM for individual countries, least developed countries on average display higher risk levels due precisely to socio-economic vulnerabilities and limited coping capacities. At the aggregate level, other developing countries, on average, exhibit higher risk levels than landlocked developing countries and small island developing States. Some countries with special needs, such as the Central Asian landlocked countries, are low-risk countries due to their high socio-economic achievemnets.

This chapter also underscores the fact that while armed conflict tends to be concentrated in a few countries, risk factors are widespread. Thus, a more dynamic assessment of conflict is warranted, as once a conflict has erupted it can easily escalate to destabilizing levels. Importantly, successful pursuit of sustainable development requires an unequivocal understanding of risk factors and the historical context that makes countries more susceptible to conflict.

ENDNOTES

[1] HAI is one of three criteria used to determine a country's least developed country status. It is a composite measure of a country's attainment in the social indicators of undernourishment, literacy, under-five mortality and gross secondary enrolment ratios. Afghanistan's score in 2015 was 43.1 against a least developed country average of 51.5 and a developing country average of 75.2.

[2] Although the Cambodian Civil War ended in 1979, low-intensity conflict continued to affect the country for more than a decade (Zasloff, 2002).

CHAPTER 3
Risk factors, conditions and triggers of conflict

In addition to having a unique history, political and cultural background, and political motivations, socio-economic and environmental stresses feature commonly in conflict-prone and conflict-ridden countries. These stresses often include income and social inequalities, also across ethnic groups, limited political representation of minorities, a rich natural resource endowment, and environmental hazards that have diverse impacts on different social groups. These conflicts are also often exacerbated by high levels of unemployment and extreme poverty, especially among young people.

Table 3.1. shows that countries at higher risk of conflict tend to perform worse across a range of development indicators. For example, conflict-prone countries often have limited fiscal space and lack foreign direct investment (FDI). They are characterized by high environmental threats to public health and ecosystems, financial exclusion and low levels of export diversification, which are typically due to high dependence on natural resources or production concentration in low value-added sectors mostly employing unskilled workers.

Although such common features are not decisive causes of conflicts, they may be linked to underlying structural elements that increase the likelihood of violent conflict and are thus defined as risk factors. Those discussed in this chapter include extreme poverty, inequality of opportunities across individuals, inequality between culturally defined groups, and natural resources. They also cover migration (internal and international) and urbanization, which can both promote stability and act as a risk factor for conflict.

Figure 3.1 illustrates a conceptual framework for understanding the links between risks factors and violent conflict. Importantly, while the existence of risk factors does not necessarily lead to violent conflicts, violence is more likely when multiple risk factors converge. Moreover, it usually takes certain bridging conditions and triggers for risk factors to develop into actual armed conflict and violence. This is particularly the case when levels of governance are poor and institutions are weak (Blattman and Miguel, 2010; World

Table 3.1. Selected socio-economic and environmental indicators for countries with special needs, average, by INFORM risk class

	INFORM risk class		
	Very high or high risk	Medium risk	Low or very low risk
GDP per capita (Current US$, 2016)	1 269	2 459	6 436
Poverty rate (Working poor living on less than US$1.90 a day, per cent of total employment [15+], 2016)	35.8	10.5	3.8
Social protection coverage (Employed population covered in the event of work injury, per cent of employed, 2013-2016)	7.8	30.4	47.2
Public health expenditure (Per cent of government expenditure, 2015)	9.1	10.6	12.5
Environmental Performance Index (2016, lower values indicate higher environmental threats)	45.3	63.5	67.7
Proportion of adults with a bank account (Per cent of adults [15+], 2015)	28.7	32.8	36.3
Tax revenue (Per cent of GDP, 2016)	12.0	18.8	18.2
Foreign direct investment inflow (Per cent of GDP, average 2011-2015)	0.6	4.4	6.2
Access to infrastructure (Asia-Pacific Infrastructure Index, 2015, lower values indicate lower accessibility)	0.17	0.28	0.38
High-technology exports (Per cent of manufactured exports, average 2011-2015)	4.3	13.5	10.8
Export diversification index (2016, higher values indicate lower diversification)	0.81	0.78	0.76

Sources: ESCAP, based on data from the United Nations Global SDGs Indicators Database, UNCTAD Stat, the World Development Indicators Database, Yale University, and ESCAP (2017a).

Note: Countries with special needs in the very high or high risk class include Afghanistan, Bangladesh, Myanmar, Nepal and Papua New Guinea; Countries with special needs in the medium risk class are Armenia, Azerbaijan, Cambodia, Kiribati, Kyrgyzstan, the Lao People's Democratic Republic, Marshall Islands, Federated States of Micronesia, Mongolia, Solomon Islands, Tajikistan, Timor-Leste, Tuvalu and Vanuatu; and those in low risk class are Bhutan, Fiji, Kazakhstan, Maldives, Nauru, Palau, Samoa, Tonga, Turkmenistan and Uzbekistan.

Bank, 2011). For example, extreme poverty and heightened vulnerable employment could cause social unrest and violence under conditions where a Government fails to deliver basic social services or economic safety-nets to protect its people and communities from adverse impacts of external shocks.

Risk factors, either socio-economic or environmental, are usually structural, as are the institutional bridging conditions. These factors create a potentially explosive situation where imbalances and economic and political grievances

are omnipresent and in which violent conflict may be triggered by external factors, such as political instability in neighbouring countries, natural disasters, climate change, and economic shocks (including commodity price shocks and terms of trade volatility).

This chapter sheds light on risk factors that may undermine peace and security within countries with special needs. It also examines bridging conditions and triggers that may translate into outbreaks of violence and instability. These factors are discussed with regard to each of the

Figure 3.1. A conceptual framework on the two-way link between risk factors and conflict

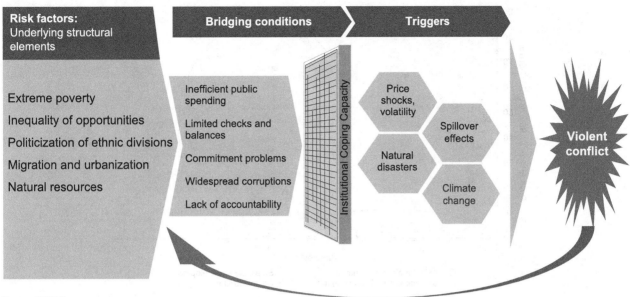

Source: ESCAP.

three dimensions of sustainable development – economic, social and environment – as well as for the institutional and political spheres.

A. Economic factors

Poverty is the most important structural element that fuels intrastate conflict. While poverty does not trigger conflict, it can increase the likelihood of the onset of conflict by, for example, creating favourable conditions for inciting violence as it is less costly to recruit the disadvantaged and the marginalized than the wealthy (Do and Iyer, 2010). Coupled with lack of employment opportunities and chronic landlessness, particularly in rural and remote areas, high rates of poverty are key in explaining the emergence of youth joining non-state forces in armed conflict. Indeed, conflict-related deaths tend to be significantly higher in poorer districts located in mountains and near forests.

Conflict in turn perpetuates poverty by destroying physical and human capital, impeding investment and innovation, and permitting weak institutions. Empirical evidence supports this two-way linkage between poverty and violent internal conflict. For example, between 1991 and 2015, about one-half of reported localized conflict incidents and

two-thirds of deaths caused by those incidents took place in countries where more than 10 per cent of the population were living in extreme poverty (Collier and Hoeffler, 2004; Fearon and Laitin, 2003). In countries with special needs, 80 per cent of incidents and 87 per cent of deaths have occurred in six countries with poverty rates above 10 per cent.[1] Indeed, there is a strong association between poverty rates and INFORM risk levels. Thus, poverty rates are low, mostly single-digit in countries with low INFORM scores, while the rates vary from 5 per cent to 80 per cent for those in the high-risk class or with high INFORM scores of above 5 (figure 3.2).

Despite the consensus that poverty is a key determinant of intrastate conflict, a multitude of complex socio-economic and political factors warrant careful country-specific analysis (Collier and others, 2003). For example, while the causality of conflict to poverty is clear since violence impairs incentives for productive economic investment and innovation, poverty as the causal mechanism for conflict can be rather ambiguous (Kanbur, 2007). Indeed, there are poor societies that are peaceful, just as there are richer societies that are mired in violence. Moreover, within countries, wealthier areas are not more immune to communal violence, arguably because wealth can sometimes provide the means for conflict.

Figure 3.2. Poverty and INFORM

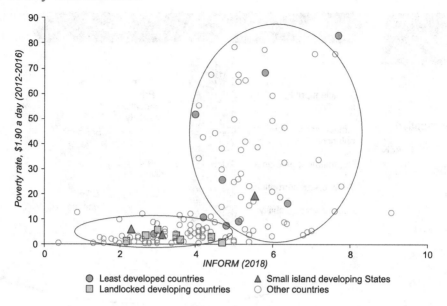

Source: ESCAP, based on data from the Global SDGs Indicators Database of the United Nations Statistics Division (available from unstats. un.org/sdgs/indicators/database/ – accessed 1 February 2018) and the Inter-Agency Standing Committee and the European Commission (available from www.inform-index.org, accessed 20 November 2017).

Note: Poverty rates refer to averages over 2012-2016 of working poor living on less than US$1.90 a day (2011 PPP) in total employment, aged 15 years and above. Available from unstats.un.org/sdgs/indicators/database/. Accessed 20 November 2017.

The relationship between poverty and conflict is stronger in States with weak institutions, as the likelihood of a rebel group's success in a civil war in such a context is higher than in a State with strong institutions (Fearon and Laitin, 2003). While the actions of Governments and their levels of corruption are important factors that influence the way poverty and conflict interact to hinder development, the impact of conflict on poverty tends to be concentrated in lagging areas within countries. Moreover, the link between poverty and conflict is reinforced by unfavourable health and education outcomes, and thus requires broader policy interventions to sustain human development (Collier and Hoeffler, 2004; Kim and Conceição, 2010).

In this context, the consequential effects of conflict on poverty, and of poverty on conflict, may be more severe in countries with special needs than in other developing countries. This is because many countries with special needs (a) have weak institutions, low capacities to cope with humanitarian crises and disasters, low levels of human development, particularly in least developed countries, and (b) often face adverse geographic and climate conditions; this is particularly the case for landlocked developing countries and small island developing States.

Due to economic grievances resulting from extreme poverty and the lack of employment opportunities, a violent conflict can be triggered by sudden economic shocks, such as food price shocks and terms of trade volatility. Changes in food prices in either direction can disrupt food security and affect the onset of violent conflict, particularly in countries where rates of poverty are high, as is the case in many countries with special needs.[2] For example, monthly spikes in international food prices have been linked to increased political unrest worldwide (Bellemare, 2015). Although a positive shock to food prices, while favouring producers, will penalize consumers, a sharp drop in food prices can also trigger conflict by deteriorating the livelihood of the poor whose income depends on agricultural products. Thus, a 20 per cent drop in food prices is estimated to lead to a 1 percentage point increase in the likelihood of civil war (Fjelde, 2015).

Terms of trade volatility may also trigger conflict. Thus, greater import prices increase conflict risk by suppressing real wages, while higher export prices may lead to greater conflict risk in countries with insufficient transparency of public revenue, as it can boost revenue thereby tempting armed groups (Besley and Persson, 2008). Calì and Mulabdic (2017) found that, among various price shocks, increases in the prices of a country's exported commodities matter the most; a 10 per cent increase in the export value raises the risk of conflict by between 2.2 and 2.5 percentage points. However, trade shocks tend to function as a trigger of conflict only where political institutions are weak (Besley and Persson, 2008).

B. Social factors

Inequalities of opportunities in terms of employment, access to health, education and other basic social services are also key drivers of conflict, especially across culturally defined groups in terms of ethnicity and religion (Bahgat

and others, 2017). Inequalities have a negative impact on social cohesion, weaken political institutions and lead to instability that, in turn, can facilitate rent-seeking, deter foreign investment and impede the domestic consensus. In societies where inequalities abound, collective action is undermined by the pursuit of the individual or vested interest groups. For example, expanding inequality of opportunities has contributed to the growing influence of extremist groups, especially among the youth in rural regions.

Using a dissimilarity index (D-index), ESCAP (2018) measures inequality of opportunities across various indicators that are critical to human wellbeing, such as access to education, health, electricity, water and sanitation. Examining how many indicators performed by a country are above average in Asia-Pacific developing countries, Afghanistan was found to perform worse than average for eight of the nine inequalities of opportunities for which data were available (figure 3.3). Kazakhstan was the best performer among countries with special needs, as it scored below average in only one measure of inequality.

Figure 3.3. Overlapping inequalities of opportunity (percentage of the 10 opportunities for which the D-index is above average)

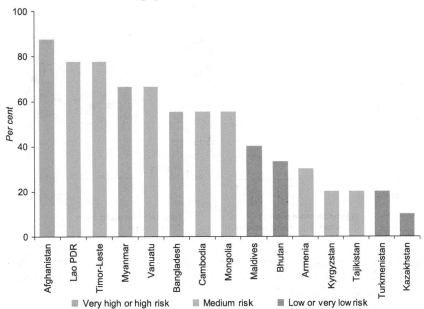

Legend: Very high or high risk   Medium risk   Low or very low risk

Sources: ESCAP (2018) and the Inter-Agency Standing Committee and the European Commission (available from www.inform-index.org, accessed 20 November 2017).

Note: Data refer to the latest survey between 2000 and 2015 for all countries in the Asia-Pacific region, where available. The orange bars are countries that bear a very high or high risk of instability, while the yellow bars are countries at medium risk, and the green bars are for those with low risk according to INFORM 2018.

Overall, countries with higher levels of inequality tend to also bear higher risks of instability, as measured by INFORM.

There is also increasing recognition that gender equality and the elimination of gender-based violence are critical to building more peaceful, inclusive and equitable societies. Gender inequality in a broader sense – whether measured in terms of wealth, labour force participation, or other human development indicators – is a more consistent indicator of high conflict risk than income inequality (bottom-right panel of figure 3.4).

Women face multiple, complex and entrenched barriers to their political, social and economic inclusion. Economic marginalization based on gender is reflected in limited opportunities for employment and decent work, a persisting gender wage gap, underrepresentation in most leadership and decision-making roles, and concentration in low status, low-paid and poorly regulated 'female' occupations. Prevalence of gender-based

Figure 3.4. INFORM and inequality of income, education, health and gender

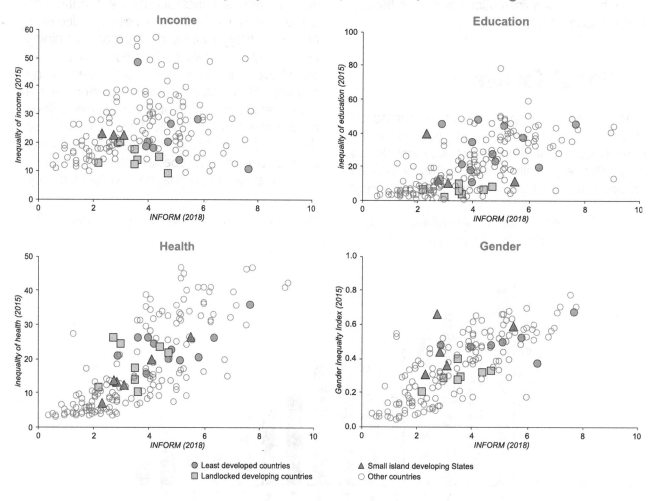

Source: ESCAP, based on data from the Inter-Agency Standing Committee and the European Commission (available at www.inform-index. org – accessed 20 November 2017) and the Human Development Index database of the United Nations Development Programme (available at hdr.undp.org/en/indicators/ – accessed 1 February 2018).

Note: Inequalities in income, education and health refer, respectively, to inequality in income distribution based on data from household surveys, inequality in distribution of expected length of life based on data from life tables, and inequality in distribution of years of schooling based on data from household surveys. These three measures are estimated using the Atkinson inequality index. Inequality in gender refers to the Gender Inequality Index, a composite measure reflecting inequality in achievement between women and men in three dimensions – reproductive health, empowerment and the labour market. For details on how the Gender Inequality Index is calculated, see hdr.undp.org/en/content/calculating-indices.

violence is a particularly disturbing manifestation of women's inequality in several small island developing States, among others, where studies have revealed high levels of domestic violence and child abuse (figure 3.5).

Importantly, domestic violence not only takes a heavy toll of the health of women and children. It also has development costs, as it results in higher absenteeism, reduced productivity and lower incomes. While such conflict is expressed within the primary unit of the family, its repercussions ultimately threaten the social fabric and cohesion that underlie peace and security. Moreover, broader social tensions and community violence arising from other sources of inequality, exclusion or injustice have tended to exacerbate women's inequality and susceptibility to violence. This has been amply demonstrated by the higher incidence of sexual assault and domestic violence associated with political and armed conflict in the region.

Income inequality does not appear to be strongly correlated with the overall levels of fragility or conflict risk. As illustrated by the top-left panel of figure 3.4, inequality is relatively low in countries in conflict, such as Afghanistan, or in

post-conflict countries, such as Cambodia. This could be explained by the destruction of capital and physical wealth, and subsequently revenue during the war, as war is often considered a major leveller of inequalities (Piketty, 2014). Another explanation for this weak association could be limited data availability and a lack of compatibility for measures of income inequality across countries. Others also argue that it is not income inequality that drives the risk of conflict; rather, structural divisions between geographic regions or ethnic or religious groups matter if income disparities align with these divisions (see, for example, Stewart, 2000).

The politicization of ethnic divisions, and those that involve faith, is also an important social risk factor for violent conflict. Indeed, most violent conflicts in countries with special needs have had an element of ethnicity, which is exploited by belligerent actors – either internal or external – and often compounded by conflicting economic incentives across social and political groups (Stewart, 2000; Hull and Imai, 2013; Ray and Esteban, 2017). Thus, according to the State Failure Problem Set database published by the Political Instability Task Force (2017), more than half of the civil conflicts recorded between

Figure 3.5. Percentage of women aged 15-49 years experiencing intimate partner physical and sexual violence, in selected small island developing States

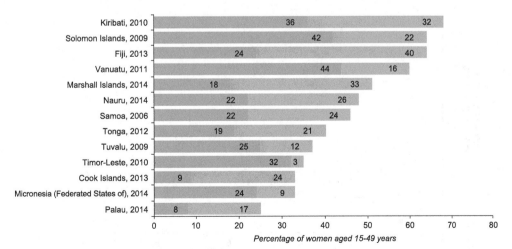

Percentage of women aged 15-49 years

▪ Ever-partnered women who have experienced intimate partner violence in past 12 months (current)
▪ Ever-partnered women who have ever experienced intimate partner violence (lifetime)

Sources: ADB (2016) and the Global Database on Violence against Women, UN WOMEN. Accessed 16 March 2018.

1955 and 2016 have been classified as ethnic. Similarly, the World Bank (2017) has found that the distribution of power among ethnic groups is a strong predictor of violent conflict. In this context, State responses to ethnic and regional discontent are a critical factor in determining whether conflicts turn violent.

However, ethnic divisions can only be a risk factor and not a trigger of conflict. Ethnic divisions become problematic only when political power centres see reasons to exploit them. In fact, there are also many ethnically diverse countries that have continued to live in peace and harmony. One of the common features of such countries is that structural divisions between geographic regions or ethnic or religious groups do not coincide with income inequality or inequality of opportunities.

International migration is an important factor, both in political and economic dimensions and has developmental consequences. It can be both a factor in the promotion of stability and a risk factor for conflict. Migration can promote stability in countries or regions of destination as it provides additional labour supply. It can reduce the potential for conflict in countries of origin where population growth is rapid or where

employment opportunities are insufficient. It can further encourage bilateral economic cooperation between countries or regions of origin and of destination. As far as the human hazard and exposure component of INFORM is concerned, however, there is no apparent systematic association between international migration and conflict risks (figure 3.6). This may be due to various factors that drive migration, either inwards or outwards, some on a voluntary basis and some with a pull from external factors.

Most countries with special needs have a net outflow of persons (figure 3.7). The largest outflows (in terms of share of population) take place from small island developing States, followed by least developed countries and landlocked developed countries. In landlocked developing countries in North and Central Asia, most emigrants migrate to the Russian Federation for employment purposes, and thus by themselves are not indicative of violent conflict. In small island developing States, most migration is in pursuit of employment or in response to the impact of climate change and climate-related hazards, notably from outer islands and from rural areas to urban centres. A household survey in Kiribati revealed that the vast majority of movements are to the capital South Tarawa, placing additional strain on an already

Figure 3.6. Net international migration rates and human hazard

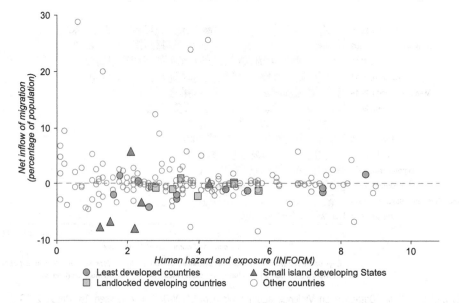

Source: ESCAP, based on data from the Inter-Agency Standing Committee, the European Commission and the World Bank (2017) Migration and Remittances Data.

Figure 3.7. Net international migration rates, percentage of population, 2015

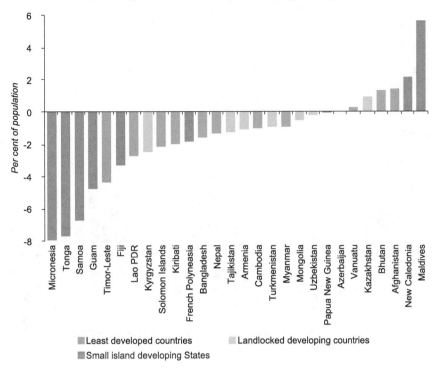

Source: World Population Prospects 2017, United Nations Department of Economic and Social Affairs. Available at esa.un.org/unpd/wpp/Download/Standard/Migration/. Accessed 21 March 2018.

fragile ecosystem and overcrowded environment. Two least developed countries, Afghanistan and Bhutan, have witnessed positive net flows. This is, in part, due to robust long-term economic growth (Bhutan) and post-conflict reconstruction (Afghanistan). Large and positive migration flows to New Caledonia and Maldives are largely due to long-term settlement from mainland France (in the case of New Caledonia) and temporary labour migration in the tourism sector from neighbouring Bangladesh and India (in the case of Maldives).

Workers' remittances constitute an important source of finance for development in recipient countries and have been recognized as a key enabler of socio-economic development in some countries. For example, Kyrgyzstan, Nepal and Tajikistan received the equivalent of more than a quarter of their respective GDP (figure 3.8). In those countries, remittances play an important role in strengthening individual and societal resilience. They have also alleviated pressure of conflict by reducing poverty. For example, remittances are estimated to have reduced the national poverty

rate by 6 to 7 percentage points between 2010 and 2013 in Kyrgyzstan, while Nepal saw a surge in remittances following the 2015 earthquake (UNDP, 2015; World Bank, 2016). Despite these economic benefits, unregulated or uncontrolled mass migration is often a source of political tension in countries or cities of destination.

Significant migration flows within a country can also increase tensions, undermine a fragile political system and contribute to militancy. Indeed, in Asia-Pacific countries with special needs, migration – either internationally or domestically – has served, among others, as a cause of an armed conflict on several occasions.

Forced migration and internal displacement due to armed conflict have led to further conflict and deterioration in development outcomes. This is because compared to the general population, refugees and internally displaced persons (IDPs) often live in markedly insecure conditions and are more vulnerable to predation and forced recruitment by non-State groups and actors.[3]

Figure 3.8. Remittance inflows as a percentage of GDP, average between 2012-2016

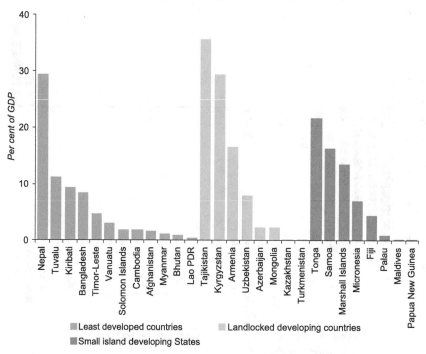

Source: Migration and Remittances Data, World Bank. Available at www.worldbank.org/en/topic/migrationremittancesdiasporaissues/brief/migration-remittances-data. Accessed 21 February 2018.

Large-scale forced returns of migrants can also be disruptive, creating challenges for countries of origin, one reason being that social welfare programmes are often unavailable in countries with special needs. Particularly in the case of returning combatants, this impedes reintegration into the community. Many countries also face growing difficulties with regard to the reintegration of their citizens who have been forcefully repatriated for criminal offences abroad. Thus, in 2016, Pacific Islands Forum Leaders highlighted the growing number of criminal deportees from metropolitan countries as an inherent security risk for the region. On average, people deported back to Samoa and Tonga had spent over 20 years outside of their birth country (Pereira, 2011). In addition to dealing with social stigma and discrimination, which often prevents employment or access to services, many returnees had poor local language skills and cultural connectedness.

Migration, that spurs competition for access to land and resources, has also resulted in violent conflicts in countries in special needs. This is particularly the case where mass migration has changed demography, culture and political

dynamics of societies of destination. For example, in Papua New Guinea, the Bougainville Civil War (1988-1998) was rooted in internal migration of the Papuans to Bougainville for the operation of copper mines. In the Solomon Islands, the increasing migration of Malaitans to Guadalcanal led to a violent conflict as the native Gwale people feared losing their traditional land.

Migration as a cause of a conflict can also directly be related to the process of urbanization and the movement of labour between agricultural and non-agricultural jobs. While urbanization contributes towards economic growth in general, it also increases pressure on social and physical infrastructure and can spark concerns over integration as well as competition for land and resources. These risks are present in many of the countries with special needs in the region, such as Bangladesh, Cambodia, Maldives and Mongolia.

Overall, migration has significant policy consequences. To ensure that migration can contribute to stability in countries or regions of destination, it is important to ensure that it takes place in a safe, orderly and regular fashion. In countries and regions of origin, Governments may opt for more liberal and open economic policies so that remittances from abroad are transferred as efficiently as possible.

C. Environmental factors

While natural resources abundance can lead to violent conflict, the link between natural resources and conflict is multi-layered and complicated. On the one hand, natural resource abundance could foster development due to potential revenue streams and alleviate socio-economic risk factors such as poverty and unemployment. Australia, Botswana, Canada and Norway all have rich natural resources and have not experienced significant violence in generations (Ross, 2015). On the other hand, rich endowment of, and dependence on high-value natural resources, can also increase the risk of violent conflict. A distinction can be observed between resource abundance and resource dependence, in that resource-dependent economies are usually less diversified and tend not to have strong labour-intensive services and manufacturing, whereas the resource-rich but less dependent and low-risk

countries mentioned above have average rents from resources of less than 5 per cent of GDP. The poor development performance of resource-rich economies has been well documented and understood as a "resource curse" (Sachs and Warner, 1995) or as "natural resource trap" (Collier, 2007). It is partly explained by Dutch disease and revenue volatility. Thus, an estimated 40-60 per cent of civil wars after the Second World War have been triggered, funded or sustained by natural resources, especially hydrocarbons (Brack and Hayman, 2006).

Given the high dependence of some landlocked developing countries on extractive industries for foreign exchange earnings, an understanding of the interlinkages among natural resources, development and conflict is critical. Figure 3.9 shows a non-linear association between resource rent-to-GDP ratios and scores of the Fragile States Index. It reveals that countries with low fragility scores tend to have low natural resource rents while many fragile States have double-digit rent-to-GDP ratios. Similarly, as far as INFORM scores are concerned, natural resource rents in countries classified as high risk are significantly higher (in terms of percentage of GDP) than in countries with medium and low risk (figure 3.10). The gaps with the other two groups

Figure 3.9. Natural resource rents as a percentage of GDP and Fragile States Index

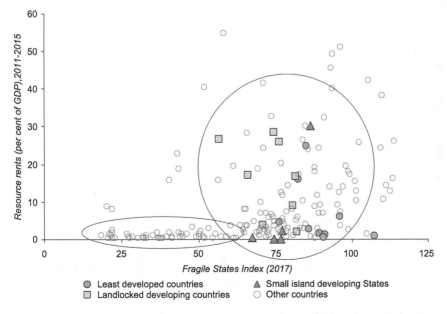

Source: ESCAP, based on data from the World Bank and the Fund for Peace.

have, in fact, increased over time as high risk countries have become more natural-resource dependent, whereas the levels of dependency of other countries has remained constant during the past three decades.

Conflict can arise from competition over resources or unfair distribution of rents, while not all types of natural resources are considered equally risky. Insurgencies and intrastate conflicts tend to flourish in countries with rich hydrocarbon or precious metal deposits because of the potentially high returns to winners and the availability of easy finance (Ross, 2004 and 2006; Collier and Hoeffler, 2004). This is partly because many resource-dependent countries have weak institutional capacity relative to their levels of per capita income and may be unable to distribute their resource rents fairly, thus causing social grievances that lead to armed conflict (Isham and others, 2005; Fearon, 2005). Weak governance in some of the resource-dependent countries, especially in terms of accountability, transparency and capability in service delivery, can be traced back to the colonial era when institutions were often set up to facilitate the transfer of resources out of the colonies (Acemoglu and others, 2001). Accordingly, they did not introduce much protection for private property, nor did

they provide checks and balances against the Government.

Furthermore, figure 3.11 shows that Governments in resource-dependent countries tend to spend less on health than do other countries. Most countries with resource rents above the 9 per cent world average have health expenditure below the world average of 11 per cent (the upper-left quadrant of figure 3.11). Notably, five of the eight Asian landlocked developing countries fall within this quadrant.

The spillover effects of exclusion from benefits, rent-seeking, corruption, poor governance and underdeveloped human capital on social cohesion has led to violent conflicts and undermined sustainable development. In Timor-Leste, the absence of an effective legal framework to determine land ownership and resource usage rights, among other factors, fuelled communal violence in 2006-2007. In Papua New Guinea, weak governance of resource-based rents has been identified as the single factor most likely to undermine prospects for sustainable growth (Avalos and others, 2015). In Kiribati, where basic development challenges related to water and sanitation persist, the Government has set enhancing governance as one of its medium-term

Figure 3.10. Natural resource rents as a percentage of GDP, by INFORM risk class

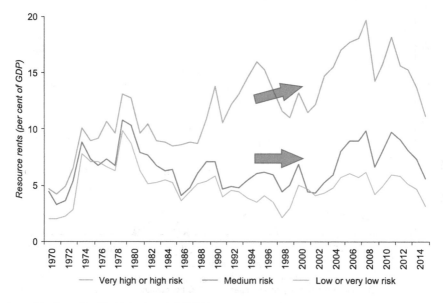

Source: ESCAP, based on data from the World Bank and INFORM.

Note: Simple averages are reported. Risk classification is based on the 2018 INFORM scores.

Figure 3.11. Natural resource rents and government expenditure on health

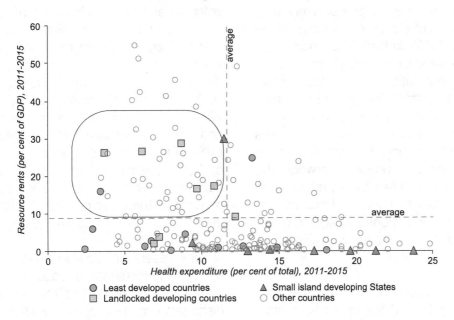

Source: ESCAP, based on data from the World Bank and the Global SDGs Indicators Database, United Nations Statistics Division.

development priorities, particularly with greater transparency and accountability in public service delivery (Government of Kiribati, 2016).

While resource abundance can be a factor contributing to conflict, resource scarcity also appears to be associated with the potential risk of conflict, particularly over the management of resources indispensable to human life and agricultural production. For example, access to freshwater can risk intra- and interstate conflict. While water-related disputes alone have rarely acted as a source of violent conflict, rapid population growth and the impact of environmental deterioration and changing climate have made freshwater scarce to the extent that insufficient water supply could cause social unrest and mass migration as well as exacerbate conditions that can lead to violent conflict and may drive people or States to fight over access. Among some of the Asian landlocked developing countries, scarcity and uneven distribution of water has resulted in conflict between upstream and downstream States (Suleimenova, 2018).

Access to land is also deeply connected to people's well-being and livelihoods, and a land shortage and unequal distribution of access and

exclusion often contribute to tensions in conflict-affected countries. For example, in Timor-Leste, the acute housing shortage for IDPs and returnees contributed to a surge in violent conflict after the peace agreement. In Nepal, grievances over landlessness and unequal distribution were also important factors that disrupted the post-conflict recovery (United Nations and World Bank, 2017; United Nations Interagency Framework Team for Preventive Action, 2012). Competition over land has been further aggravated by environmental degradation, urbanization, population growth and climate change in many countries with special needs.

Natural disasters

Natural disasters can trigger and aggravate social conflict, especially in the absence of disaster risk reduction measures. Indeed, approximately 70 per cent of reported conflict incidents in Asia and the Pacific occurred within earthquake hazard fault areas and approximately 84 per cent of reported incidents occurred within drought-affected areas (ESCAP, 2017d). This association exists partly because disasters trigger conflict that originates in poverty and inequality. The poor, who are forced to live in disaster prone areas, are most likely to lose their livelihoods due to disasters. In addition, underprivileged groups may face unequal distribution of aid, which can exacerbate tensions (Ferris, 2010). Indeed, in countries that historically have experienced significant conflict there is a strong correlation between the number of conflict incidents and disaster-related deaths each year, suggesting that conflict can weaken the resilience of communities and that disasters can create fertile ground for conflict. There is also a significant correlation between the number of people affected by disasters each year and the number of conflict-related deaths. These significant correlations highlight drought as a specific area of concern with regard to the conflict-disaster nexus.

Many countries with special needs, especially small island developing States, are highly vulnerable to extreme weather-related events. On average, annual direct losses caused by natural disasters are estimated at US$284 million or 1.7 per cent of their aggregate GDP (World Bank, 2013). Between 2013 and 2017, the small island developing States experienced a number of extreme weather-related

events, such as floods, storms, earthquakes and volcanic activities, with seven of these events having significant humanitarian consequences that had an impact on more than a quarter of the total population of the six affected countries (figure 3.12). For example, category 5 tropical cyclone Pam that struck the region in March 2015 was estimated to have caused damage and losses in Vanuatu that amounted to almost US$450 million, equating to about 64.1 per cent of GDP (Government of Vanuatu, 2015), while category 5 tropical cyclone Winston inflicted damage in the order of US$1.3 billion or 31 per cent of GDP in Fiji (Government of Fiji, 2016).

Natural disasters could also trigger violent conflict through interpersonal violence. This could pose a threat to communities that are affected by disasters because of (a) mental distress originating from the feelings of loss and powerlessness, and (b) increased vulnerability of women and children due to the scarcity of basic provisions and a gap in the social protection. According to some estimates, between one-third and one-half of all persons who are affected by natural disasters

Figure 3.12. People affected by extreme weather-related events in small island developing States, 2013-2017

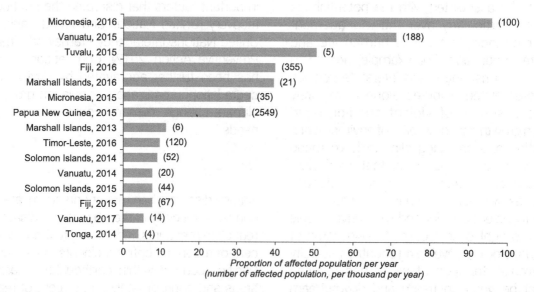

Sources: ESCAP, based on data from the International Disaster Database, Centre for Research on the Epidemiology of Disasters and the World Population Prospects Database, United Nations Department of Economic and Social Affairs. Accessed 16 March 2018.

Note: The annual number of victims for each country is calculated by adding the numbers of persons killed and persons affected and requiring immediate food, water, shelter, sanitation or medical assistance. Extreme weather-related events include hydrological, climatologic and meteorological disasters such as floods, landslides, storms, droughts and extreme temperatures as well as geophysical disasters such as earthquakes or volcanoes.

experience mental distress such as post-traumatic stress disorder, depression and anxiety disorders (WHO, 2001). Such a significant health impact will undoubtedly also have a long-term effect on individuals' level of vulnerability to violence.

This is a cause for concern, as climate change is likely to contribute to tensions and conflict in the Asia-Pacific region. Climate change will usher in incidences of saltwater intrusion, prolonged heavy rainfall and flooding, increased temperature, drought and more violent tropical cyclones. These physical changes can lead to disruption of water resources, declines in crop yields and food stocks, reduced fishery catches and severe disease outbreaks (Mazo, 2010). A prominent example of conflict that was partly triggered by climate change, although not in the Asia-Pacific region, is the war in Darfur, Sudan, which broke out in 2003. Amid growing social and ethno-political tensions as well as persistent risks of military conflict, violence began as an ecological crisis, triggered in part by climate change, environmental degradation and unsustainable population growth (UNEP, 2007). Indeed, strong historical linkages between the onset of civil war and rises in temperature have been found in Africa, with warmer years leading to significant increases in the likelihood of war (Burke and others, 2009).

Thus, climate change and the resulting shortages of water and food have the potential for triggering conflicts, particularly those over access to resources. This is particularly pertinent to Asia-Pacific least development countries, landlocked developing countries and small island developing States. Indeed, the Government of Bangladesh has recognized in its Climate Change Strategy and Action Plan the need to prepare for an influx of people from low-elevated coastal areas into large cities as a result of climate change. Kiribati has already adopted a "migration with dignity" policy to urge its citizens to consider moving abroad because of the effects of climate change. Box 3.1 illustrates the climate-conflict nexus, based on the experiences of the landlocked developing countries in the North and Central Asian subregion.

D. Institutional and political factors

Spillover effects usually have significant international consequences that could be both positive and negative, as they often affect bilateral relations between countries. International spillover effects of domestic political events, which lead to violent conflicts, are not uncommon. This is particularly the case when countries share geographic proximity, a history of interaction, and similar institutional and systemic arrangements. These spillovers may have significant impact on development trajectories of States, as they influence their organization, functioning and capabilities. It is thus possible for a violent conflict in one country to trigger similar events in another, or for an extensive systemic reformulation in one country to lead the people in another to demand changes. For spillover effects to trigger a violent conflict in another country, it would require matured domestic conditions created by the presence of risk factors.

Historically, spillover effects have played an important role in countries with special needs in shaping institutions and policies as well as inciting violent conflict. Contemporarily, the spillover effects are still visible among countries with special needs and often go beyond their borders, as the developmental impact of intercommunal instability in Myanmar's Rakhine State on neighbouring Bangladesh has demonstrated (Annan, 2017), with the influx of refugees currently constituting around 0.4 per cent of Bangladesh's population of approximately 160 million. Similarly, the conflict in Afghanistan is having an adverse impact on security and development in neighbouring countries.

As for bridging conditions, violent conflict generally does not take place if a country has a functioning framework of viable rules that govern the allocation of resources and a peaceful settlement mechanism of potential grievances, even if that country possesses large resource

Box 3.1. Climate change and water security in North and Central Asia

In Central Asia and the Caucasus, climate change-related risks are somewhat similar – i.e., the disruption of water resources and the reduction of long-term water reserves. According to various climate change scenarios, assessment of the change in water regime in members of the Commonwealth of Independent States, including Central Asia and the Caucasus, reveals that water stocks will decline further in those areas that are already experiencing scarcity. At the same time, declines in precipitation during summer will threaten food security, while increases in average temperatures will make habitats less comfortable for living (Blinov, 2012).

In Central Asia, climate change is particularly linked to freshwater supply and long-term water reserves, i.e., the glaciers. Climate change is likely to reduce water resources in the northern plains of Central Asia by 6-10 per cent by 2030, and an additional 4-8 per cent by 2050 (Ibatullin, 2013), mainly due to the increased losses in runoff and infiltration as well as the reduction in snow accumulation. Degradation of glaciers will result in a reduction of water resources in mountainous areas by 10-12 per cent, which will in turn decrease run-off in summer – the irrigation period – and increase the likelihood of flooding in spring (Ibatullin, 2013). Potentially, such variations in water stocks and flow may intensify competition and tension over water resources. Coupled with growing water demand stemming from economic development and population growth, this will increase pressure on existing resources. With high population growth, especially in the Fergana Valley, the water-intensive cotton production may remain a chief sector of employment in the foreseeable future, hence water consumption is unlikely to be reduced (Hanks, 2010).

In the Caucasus, climate change has the potential to threaten the availability of freshwater resources and may undermine the prospect of economic development and human security of States.

Existing conflict undermines effective cooperation and actions on climate change adaptation and mitigation in the region. Moreover, reduced water availability due to climate change may also have a negative impact on the internal stability of States. For example, water stress caused by climate change will have severe implications for the lifestyles of people living in areas dependent on agriculture of arid and semi-arid zones; it could pose a serious threat to the livelihood of the marginalized groups and is therefore linked to human security issues (Mobjörk and others, 2016).

While the shrinking of the Aral Sea cannot be directly linked to climate change, it provides an example of the potential risks associated with changes in lifestyles of communities due to environmental degradation and disruption of water resources. The decimation of fisheries with catches declining from 40,000 tons in 1960 to nothing in 1980, left about 60,000 people jobless (Glantz and Zonn, 2005).

The decline in economic activity contributed to a significant increase in the level of diseases, including outbreaks of waterborne infectious diseases, including typhoid, hepatitis A and diarrhoea, and the spread of tuberculosis and respiratory diseases. In addition, the Aral Sea region has the highest rate of anaemia, while infant mortality rates in the basin increased from about 25 per 1,000 live births in 1950 to 70-100 per 1,000 in 1996 (Whish-Wilson, 2002).

In sum, "[the] multi-causal nature of the climate-security nexus works both ways. While climate change may act as a threat multiplier in conjunction with political, economic or social factors, such factors can reduce the ability of a society to implement measures to mitigate effects of environmental impacts of climate change, thus acting as threat multipliers for environmental stresses" (Mazo, 2010). At the same time, these factors will not seriously disrupt the order and activity in the States, where the adaptive and problem-solving capacity is well-enforced.

Source: Suleimenova, 2018.

rents. This is because there are various options available for conflict alleviation, management of pre-conflict situations and resolution. Thus, risks and violent conflicts can be bridged only under certain conditions, particularly when the quality of governance for conflict alleviation is poor.

Weak institutions and widespread corruption, especially among the elite, are imperative to explaining the development of a dissident organization and the realization of violent conflict (Gurr, 1971). Thus, disorder can result from the weakening of enforcement of rules or norms of cooperation, which induces organizations to demand radical changes (North, 2006). The onset of various internal armed conflicts is often preceded by years of political factionalism, lack of socio-economic opportunities and weak institutions that have been unable to address diverging aspirations and expectations of the population and the plight of poor. Figure 3.13 further confirms that better governance is associated with lower levels of conflict risks and vulnerabilities.

In this context, good governance is critical in preventing violence through its impact on resolving disputes over socio-economic risks such as extreme poverty and inequalities in opportunities. Governance quality can have a significant impact on the level of social protection and health and education outcomes. It can improve the quality of infrastructure because of the critical role of governance in the efficiency and effectiveness of public spending (ESCAP, 2017b). Likewise, higher public spending on health and education has little impact in countries with weak governance (Rajkumar and Swaroop, 2008), thus underscoring the critical role of governance in navigating conflict peacefully.

Good governance can facilitate compromise between competing groups by providing opportunities for transparent information exchange through dialogue and negotiation. It also ensures enforcement of commitment decisions by state institutions intertemporally. Thus, if a State decides not to follow a previously agreed resource management system due to a change in that country's political interests and economic priorities, the natural resource risk could then lead to conflict. Box 3.2 provides a theoretical background on how information asymmetry and commitment problems caused by weak institutions could set up conditions for violent conflict.

Figure 3.13. Correlation between governance and conflict risks and vulnerability

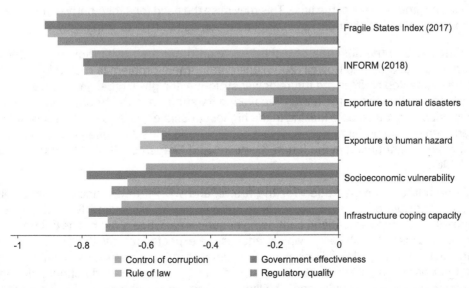

Source: ESCAP, based on data from the Fund for Peace Fragile States Index 2017, INFORM 2018 and the World Bank Worldwide Governance Indicators database, 2016.

Box 3.2. Information asymmetry, commitment problems and weak institutions

Theoretically, for a violence conflict to erupt, expected payoffs of conflict must be perceived to exceed expected costs of conflict by at least one of the parties involved. If a bargained solution is as effective as the hard-won reward for war, rational agents should prefer bargaining rather than waging a war. However, conflict among rational agents takes place far more frequently because they find violent events unavoidable in cases where negotiation is neither feasible nor desirable, possibly due to an institution's lack of capacity to mediate effective bargaining.

Theoretical works with a focus on the reasons why bargaining would fail highlight information asymmetry and commitment problems as the mechanisms behind these bargaining failures.

Information asymmetry is one of the conditions that can lead to bargaining failures and thus conflict. This argument explains that rational leaders may be unable to make a mutually beneficial settlement because they have the incentive to mispresent private information (Fearon, 1995). Leaders have private information regarding their military power and will take the risk of mispresenting this private information as long as they can broker a better deal. This will, in turn, lead to the opponent's miscalculation due to the provision of poor information. Recent literature provides much relevant evidence of information asymmetry's role by showing that mediation, which solves asymmetric information by providing critical knowledge about the disputants' positions, is the most effective way of managing violent conflicts (Rauchhaus, 2006). In other words, when all parties are aware of what they can and cannot gain from each other, there will be no need to deter their opponents by exaggerating their capabilities.

While information asymmetry provides valuable insights into the cause of bargaining failures, commitment problems mostly account for any prolonged conflicts (Fearon, 1995). They arise, for example, when a previously agreed resource management system does not fit into a country's political interests and economic priorities. The natural resource risks could then become interstate conflict if a country decides not to follow the existing agreement. The commitment problem may also directly result in a civil conflict in societies with weak government institutions as well as limited checks and balances to control executive power, since formal legal and state institutions are believed to help in enforcing commitments intertemporally (see, for example, Fearon and Laitin, 2003; La Ferrara and Bates, 2001; Skaperdas, 2008). In fact, it is argued that conflict may be unavoidable, as societies are often composed of multiple groups, and it is impossible to find arrangements that will satisfy all the groups at the same time. This may raise the need for a third-party enforcer, even though the effects of external intervention could have various outcomes (see, for example, Ray, 2009).

Yet, weak institutions and the absence of a third-party enforcer are not sufficient conditions for the outbreak of conflicts. According to Powell (2006), the commitment problem is rooted in expectations for the future, such as expected shifts in the future power structure. If a given rebel group expects that a weak Government will not stick to the bargain after recovering its strength in the future, it will be interested in continuing a violent conflict to secure locking in the highest possible gains as early as possible. Similarly, a central Government would prefer to fight a violent conflict if the impact resulted in the weakening of the rebel group for a significant period in the future (Garfinkel and Skaperdas 2000; McBride and Skaperdas, 2007; Powell, 2006).

Another condition related to expectation for the future, and which may cause a violent conflict, is a deteriorating economic outlook. A negative economic outlook may be associated, for example, with reports of extensive growth in unemployment and continuing negative real wage growth. The outlook coupled, for example, with low access to health care – which reduces the expected returns to production – decreases the opportunity cost of rebellion. In addition, while the contest model narrows the behaviour of individuals to either fighting or producing, the opportunity cost of fighting in the real world should also include the expected benefits of schooling. Populations who live in poverty or conditions of high inequality may also receive education, if schooling is widely available or is mandatory. Thus, provision of education can work as an important factor that prevents violence; higher levels of secondary school attainment are associated with a lower risk of civil war (Collier and Hoeffler, 1998 and 2004).

E. Conclusion

Conflict risks in countries with special needs are rooted in a variety of factors, ranging from poverty to inequalities in opportunities, resources and movements of people. While poverty reduction and economic growth are important, social inequality and exclusion from access to opportunities, basic social services and infrastructure, especially across gender as well as different ethnicities and religions, play a key role in modern intrastate and non-State conflicts.

Governments are primarily responsible for preventing conflict from becoming violent. As countries with special needs often suffer from weak institutions, improved government accountability – with revenue transparency and expenditure scrutiny – and a fair use of resource incomes for development and security would be useful in reducing conflict risks.

Since these risk factors are multidimensional, risk mitigation must also be multidimensional in nature. Inclusive development can be a powerful tool for prevention in this context. Providing equal opportunities across different ethnic groups, enhancing the meaningful participation of women in decision-making, and addressing grievances arising from movements of people, goods and capital would provide an effective means of sustaining peace and stability.

ENDNOTES

[1] Countries with special needs with more than 10 per cent of the population living on less than $1.90 per day are Afghanistan, Bangladesh, Cambodia, Myanmar, the Lao People's Democratic Republic, Papua New Guinea and Timor-Leste. Data are taken from the Global SDGs Indicators Database, United Nations Statistics Division, and the Uppsala Conflict Data Program. Poverty rates refer to averages during 2012-2016 of working poor living on less than US$1.90 a day (2011 PPP), in total employment, and aged 15 years and above. Timor-Leste was excluded from the analysis because the Uppsala Conflict Data Program does not report conflict data from that country.

[2] Brinkman and Hendrix (2011) and Weinberg and Bakker (2015) argued that the critical component of the food price-conflict relationship was not a result of the level of the price, but of the price change.

[3] Internally displaced persons (IDPs) are prime candidates for becoming refugees or international migrants in the future, given that a large number of refugees started their journey from their home countries as IDPs. Afghanistan accounts for the largest share of migrants with more than 1.55 million IDPs and more than 2 million refugees. In Myanmar, intercommunal violence and intensified conflict in Rakhine State have evolved into a humanitarian crisis. In September 2017, around half a million people were displaced as they fled to makeshift camps in Bangladesh. See Annan (2017) and http://www.rakhinecommission.org/app/uploads/2017/08/FinalReport_Eng.pdf.

CHAPTER 4
Policy recommendations

Economic and social policies as well as institutional and systemic modifications are integral components of the set of solutions for sustaining peace and for achieving sustainable development in the region's countries with special needs. Various development-related policies serve the purpose of preventing conflict and sustaining peace; however, this chapter focuses on those policies that specifically address the higher vulnerability level of countries with special needs.

A. Employment

While the linkages between conflict and unemployment are complex and multifaceted, youth unemployment is undoubtedly an important explanatory factor of insurgency or civil war (Cincotta and others, 2003; Heinsohn, 2003; Urdal, 2004). One reason is that when the supply of employment opportunities relative to labour market entrants is high, the opportunity cost of violence is higher, thereby making rebel recruitment challenging (Collier and Hoeffler, 2004). However, more recent studies that have attempted to shed light on the causal links have been confronted by the lack of disaggregated data. Importantly, the fact that the labour market, unlike goods and services markets, is a human social phenomenon that makes it more of a social institution (Solow, 1991) complicates any exercise to derive a primarily straightforward economic explanation. Despite the inconclusive outcome of attempts to identify causal linkages, there is a consensus that *"people's experience of labour markets often plays an important role in their participation in violence"* (Cramer, 2010). Thus, a sustainable solution for conflict prevention and durable peace must incorporate the role of employment in preventing conflict as well as the implications that conflict has for employment and labour markets.

It is not simply the unavailability of employment opportunities that may induce resorting to violence, but also the conditions of employment. Conflict, in turn, can give rise to precarious and insecure forms of employment. More specifically, during conflicts the number of people engaged in informal employment tends to increase (Looney, 2006). These outcomes are further compounded by the low levels of social protection in fragile contexts where a Government does not have the capacity to provide basic social services (Ovadiya and others, 2015). Thus, conflicts can have an impact on the demand and supply of labour. Conflict can affect the supply of labour in dichotomous ways. On the one hand, the supply of labour may increase in response to economic compulsion or the absence of members participating in conflict; on the other hand, supply could decrease due to the risks associated with participating in employment in a hostile and insecure environment. For example, three key deficits that explain the shortfall in private sector demand for labour have been highlighted in an analysis of employment in South Asia's conflict zones: (a) a stability deficit due to a lack of security of life and property; (b) a governance deficit that leads to a poor regulatory framework; and (c) an infrastructure deficit that deters economic activity (Iyer and Santos, 2012).

A combination of a high supply of labour and low demand by the private sector can result in very low wages, further deepening the downward spiral of poor employment conditions and conflict. The situation is particularly pronounced in the Asia-Pacific region, where significant demographic shifts can be observed. In Asia and the Pacific, and, more specifically, in countries with special needs a variety of trends that are of consequence for conflict can be discerned. First, these groups of countries are experiencing an ongoing or impending peak in the share of their working-age people in the total population (figure 4.1).

Such demographic shifts can have far-reaching implications for human development, with estimates of the "demographic dividend" yielding an additional 0.73 percentage points to annual output growth (UNDP, 2016a). However, to ensure that the demographic dividend does not become a demographic burden, Governments will have to proactively formulate appropriate policy choices. Sustained investment in human development would be required to harness the demographic window of opportunity. At the macroeconomic level, inclusive and high-quality economic growth and investment in human capabilities must be pursued, as failure to do so will put social stability at risk.

Figure 4.1. Rising working-age populations in Asia-Pacific countries with special needs

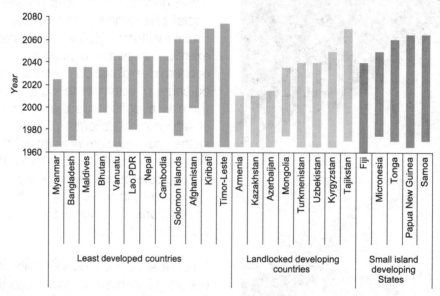

Source: ESCAP, adapted from the Asia Pacific Human Development Report 2016 and based on data from the World Population Prospects Database, United Nations Department of Economic and Social Affairs. Accessed 21 March 2018.

Note: The length of the columns depicts the years when the working age population in a country is rising. While in some years the working age population decreases marginally, these minor deviations are ignored; only the end of the trend is considered once the share in a country reaches its ultimate peak.

Second, an alarming trend in Asia and the Pacific shows that employment growth has not been commensurate with high economic growth (figure 4.2). This is further aggravated by an increase in vulnerable employment characterized by low earnings and low productivity as well as poor working conditions that undermine rights (ESCAP, 2017e). The employment deficit is particularly acute in South Asia, and more critically in conflict settings.

Employment and conflict have profound implications for each other at all stages of conflict – prior to and after a crisis as a preventive force, by keeping potential and former combatants gainfully engaged, and during conflict when vulnerability rises. Strategies to generate decent and productive employment should therefore also be contingent on the stage of conflict. While the imperative for SDG 8 is applicable to all countries, those trapped in or recovering from conflict must go the extra mile in incorporating issues related to security and vulnerability.

It is also important to underscore the fact that the workforce in high-conflict areas is more likely to be based in rural areas, and thus its employment is probably concentrated in the agrarian sector (Iyer and Santos, 2012). This is evidently the case in Afghanistan where 71 per cent of those employed in high conflict areas are in the agriculture sector, compared with 52 per cent for the rest of the country. In the case of Nepal, the employment statistics are 87 per cent and 78 per cent, respectively. Such conditions perhaps result from another related pattern observed in conflict settings, i.e., conflict may delay structural transformation.

These interrelated issues suggest that generating decent and gainful employment should begin within the rural agrarian domain. Given the largely informal nature of economic activity, critical inputs such as micro-finance and training should be tailored to such conditions in order to support self-employment opportunities (Iyer and Santos, 2012). The public sector plays an important role by providing labour-intensive public infrastructure projects that can achieve the twin goals of short-term employment generation and longer-term productive capacity-building. Successful cases include Afghanistan's decentralized community-

Figure 4.2. Growth of employment and GDP, average annual percentage change between 2000 and 2016

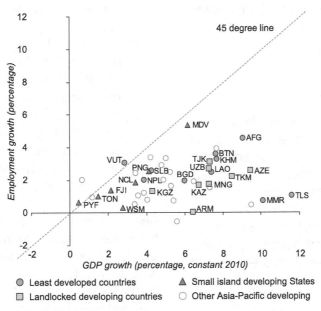

Source: ESCAP, based on data from the ESCAP Statistical Database. Accessed 21 March 2018.

Note: Growth rates presented are compound annual growth rates between 2000 and 2016. Country names and codes are available in the explanatory notes.

driven National Solidarity Programme that uses international funds for local infrastructure projects, and Nepal's Poverty Alleviation Fund that is focused on rural community infrastructure.

However, as the public sector's ability to absorb labour will inevitably become saturated, establishing complementary policies to accelerate private sector development will be necessary. Two innovative approaches have been proposed to alleviate such concerns. Akin to the concept of Special Economic Zones, the creation of Safe Economic Zones in conflict settings is being explored. Such an effort would enable a resource-constrained Government that is unable to provide security to businesses across a geographically dispersed area to consolidate its resources and efforts in a confined setting. Businesses that are particularly labour-intensive could be incentivized in such locations. However, this would be an interim measure as economic dynamism must gradually permeate other sections of a conflict-afflicted society in order to ensure durable peace. A second approach proposes community partnerships with the private sector to provide security, as in the case of Afghanistan's largest mobile phone company, Roshan. A community-based security arrangement has resulted in mutually beneficial outcomes of job creation and infrastructure for the communities on the one hand, and lower costs for more reliable security on the other.

B. Inequality

It is difficult to underestimate the role of education and health care in development and, indirectly, in sustaining peace. Better and accessible education and better health care contribute to higher levels of development. Equal access to good education creates opportunities for all to prosper, regardless of their economic status, and thus contributes to reducing inequalities and sustaining peace. Consequently, policies related to inequality of opportunity should include:

(a) Establishing a universal health-care system that is properly funded and that guarantees adequate access for all; and

(b) Providing free education for all at the primary and secondary levels.

To sustain peace, it is important that the distribution of health and educational facilities include rural and impoverished urban areas. It is also important to ensure that the quality of services does not differentiate between the affluent and impoverished areas. For countries with special needs, the problem lies not only in proper financing but also in political will and understanding that empowerment is a recipe for sustaining peace.

Throughout history, ethnic and religious diversity has been a common feature in many nations and societies. However, ethnicity and religion are often used by political power centres to incite violent conflicts. State policies to mitigate ethnicity and religion being used as triggers for violence should include:

(a) A legal code and its enforcement for preventing discrimination of ethnic and religious minorities in the labour market and in access to social services such as education and health care. These policies should not only address the socio-economic aspects of minority groups, but should also deal with common xenophobia, racism and hatred;

(b) Educational programmes on ethnic and religious diversity and their contribution to society, as part of education curricula at the primary and secondary level; and

(c) Policies to empower ethnic and religious minorities to preserve their cultural heritage and traditions, and to ensure adequate financing mechanisms for supporting this empowerment.

Gender discrimination is perhaps the longest-lasting horizontal inequality in the history of mankind. Gender equality is an intrinsic "good" in its own right, to which the international community has committed itself through, for example, Goal 5 of the 2030 Agenda for Sustainable Development. It is vital that gender gaps are bridged in labour force participation, entrepreneurship, pay and working conditions to achieve gender equality (ESCAP,

2017c). Government actions to ensure affordable elderly and child-care facilities, better and safer transport, and greater flexibility in working time and opportunities for working from home, together with comprehensive social security coverage, are important components of efforts to achieve Goal 5. Other important components include gender parity in education and guaranteeing women's equal rights to ownership, and control of land, property and other resources, alongside equal rights to inheritance. Policy recommendations for more efficient assessment of women's situation, and to empower women, also include: (a) adopting gender mainstreaming as a mechanism to enact gender-responsive policies and interventions; (b) conducting systems mapping within and across sectors to address gender concerns; (c) adopting gender budgeting to establish gender-responsive financing goals, processes and mechanisms; and (d) fostering women's participation, leadership and involvement in decision-making at all levels (ESCAP, 2017c).

C. Migration

Migration can be an important risk factor of conflict, a consequence of conflict, and a measure for sustaining peace and preventing conflict from occurring. Remittances from migrant workers abroad to individuals and families in migrants' home States are particularly relevant for many countries with special needs as they effectively lessen the financial burden of Governments in relation to social protection and job creation. To maximize the developmental gains of remittances, Governments can encourage transfers through domestic financial institutions to incentivize sectoral development. Migrants' country of origin can also create an institutional and regulatory environment to strengthen the use of remittances domestically for development-related purposes, for example, through diaspora bonds or by enabling small enterprises to access the bonds. Diaspora bonds could serve Asia-Pacific countries with special needs that have sizable populations living abroad, and where remittances are particularly sizable, as is the case for Afghanistan, Bangladesh, Kyrgyzstan, Myanmar, Nepal, Tajikistan and Tonga.

Doing so requires a transparent, corruption-free environment with simple business procedures and a level playing field, particularly in the case of small and medium-sized enterprises (SMEs). In most cases this also means eliminating various non-tariff barriers and other obstacles for small business development.

Migration can also generate significant social and political tension. To reduce these tensions, state policies should support incoming populations and provide them with necessary basic services such as shelter, health-related assistance and education. Depending on the character of the crisis, policies may aim at assimilation with the host society, while at the same time guarding the freedom to cultivate separate traditions and customs that do not violate the host country's legal norms. They may also aim at incorporating migrants into the local labour market through effective job creation strategies in the territories of the influx.

However, most countries with special needs lack the capacity and resources to do so without diverting already scarce resources from the host population. Thus, substantial financial assistance from the international community may be required to supplement domestic assistance, in order to assimilate the incoming populations or to create conditions for their safe return home. It is important that the international community's assistance is geared towards increasing the long-term capacities of a host country and the migrant population. Naturally, the international community's first role is assisting in preventing the migration crisis from happening.

D. Environment and natural disasters

Management of natural resources is a critical challenge for countries that are rich in high-value natural resources and for those facing diminishing renewable resources such as land and water.

Mitigation of conflict risks requires better governance, particularly in the context of transparency and accountability in resource management. Governance in resource-rich countries can be improved by, for example, establishing fiscal rules to report, manage and use revenues from natural resources, giving special attention to mitigating the social and environmental impacts of extractive projects. Publication of financial reporting, open access to fiscal information – such as resource revenue received – and timely audits of Government entities responsible for the delivery of public services, including state-owned enterprises, can contribute to greater transparency. Governments may also benefit from taking part in the global norm-setting efforts, such as the Extractive Industries Transparency Initiative (EITI), an agency to promote open and accountable management of natural resources. In the long-term, a conflict risk arising from natural resources can be mitigated by reducing resource dependency. Strategic diversification through the selective promotion of new economic activities with targeted industrial, infrastructural, trade and investment polies may be required if market incentives alone are inefficient to foster diversification (ESCAP, 2015).

In countries with scarce and diminishing resources, a system of checks and balances within Governments can mitigate risks of commitment problems associated with intertemporal inconsistency of public policy (Suleimenova, 2018). The system should also ensure enforcement of legal frameworks, and a transparent process for defining property rights and access to resources. If risk factors are already present, benefit sharing is a solution to overcome the contentious issue related to property rights. While operationalization of actual benefit sharing will require a combination of negotiations, cooperation and agreements, conducting a comprehensive analysis on benefits and costs of benefit sharing is a first step towards operationalization (Suleimenova, 2018). Negotiations may involve an issue-linkages strategy, under which shared benefits of resources are linked with non-resource-based issues and negotiated as a package deal. The linkages can be made in relation to financial resources, energy resources, political and other trade linkages that will encourage positive-sum solutions.

Enhanced disaster-risk reduction strategies that consider the interplay between disasters and conflict are essential to ensuring that natural disasters do not trigger conflict. Often, least developed countries, small island developing States and other low-elevated coastal zones lack adequate infrastructure to prevent hazards. Strategies must therefore be developed based on the premise that social tensions must be tackled during normal times before being exacerbated by natural disasters. Disaster-risk reduction and management need to address specific risk factors of violent conflict that countries are facing now, while also providing immediate assistance to address issues related to human rights, refugees, IDPs, extreme poverty and interpersonal violence, particularly against women.

In addition, enhancing the applications of frontier technologies, such as space technology and geographic information systems (GIS), can provide far-reaching solutions for effective early warning of disasters as well as mitigate the drivers and risks of conflict, thereby contributing to crisis prevention and sustainable development. This could be relevant, for example, in the case of drought affecting agriculture usually characterized by a slow onset disaster with prolonged dry spells, and which may result in forced migration to non-drought-prone areas, triggering conflicts and humanitarian crisis.

E. Financing for peace

Implementing the policy recommendations above requires effective mechanisms of financing for peace. Public finance, including tax policy and public expenditure management, are vital for sustaining peace. For example, greater expenditure in social sectors would reduce levels of extreme poverty and could mitigate risks of humanitarian crises and disasters. Tax policies can reduce inequalities and promote investment.

Asia-Pacific countries with special needs, however, have low tax revenue levels – averaging around 15.8 per cent of GDP compared with 17.6 per cent for the rest of the region and 18.5 per cent for the rest of the world.[1] Therefore, building more effective, efficient and accountable tax systems must remain the region's top priority. These systems must guarantee a systematic broadening of the tax base and an effective shift of the financing burden to more affluent parts of the society. Targeted and progressive taxation, combined with the right blend of public spending on social and environmental benefits, are also essential for ensuring shared prosperity and for reducing inequalities, which are critical to sustaining peace.

Most countries with special needs tend to rely on indirect taxes with a lower redistributive impact. Indeed, the share of direct personal, corporate income or wealth taxes, which have greater equity implications, remains low at 33.3 per cent of total tax revenue in countries with special needs, and 45.9 per cent for the rest of the region. This is significantly below the OECD average of 55.8 per cent. Thus, there is a clear need to employ state policies that will increase the share of direct taxes and significantly increase their redistributive impact.

Greater tax revenues are also required in order to close infrastructure gaps in countries with special needs. This is important, considering the fact that sustainable and resilient infrastructure is effective in mitigating conflict risks and sustaining peace by providing access to basic social and infrastructure services. Indeed, improved road connectivity and information and communications technology (ICT) infrastructure can significantly enhance the capacity of societies to cope with crises and disasters and thus contribute further to sustaining peace. Yet, while public finance is a key to sustainable development and peace building, catalysing private capital and expertise is critical when considering the fact that countries with special needs must spend an estimated 10.5 per cent of their GDP annually to close the development gap in infrastructure (ESCAP, 2017a).

As a practical way to engage private capital for infrastructure financing, public-private partnerships (PPPs) offer great promise. While many countries in the region are in the process of developing the necessary legal, regulatory and institutional frameworks for PPP transactions, government capacity constraints to structuring and implementing these transactions stand in the way, particularly in efforts to introduce adequate transparency, good governance and proper oversight. Deeper and more integrated capital markets could also support private sector infrastructure projects by deepening the pools of capital available to support long-term investments, innovative financing solutions and private sector credit enhancement instruments. This, however, requires greater harmonization of the regulatory architecture governing financial markets and services across the region.

Notwithstanding the importance of strengthening public finances, in many countries with special needs official development assistance (ODA) will continue to play an important role in financing sustainable development. ODA is particularly important for countries that exhibit high-risk levels of descending into conflict, as these are typically even more constrained by low levels of domestic resources for pursuing sustainable development. In particular, their lacklustre economic performance that results in a lower taxable base is compounded by weak resource mobilization efforts or corruption. Thus, an understanding of the current landscape of ODA in the context of peace and security is critical (box 4.1).

Overall, building and sustaining peace together with sustainable development are long-term endeavours that require a stable and coherent framework of development cooperation, especially in fragile States. Notwithstanding the fact that the vested political and economic interests of donors may address important and legitimate development predicaments, assistance must be more aligned with recipient countries' long-term developmental necessities. Indeed, at the international level, there is increasing recognition that *"development cooperation in fragile States differs fundamentally from engagement with 'normal developing countries' and that success requires that aid donors and recipients alike 'do things differently' by designing aid interventions that reflect the unique context of fragility in each State"* as agreed at the Fourth High Level Forum on Aid Effectiveness (OHRLLS, 2013). This is especially important considering

Box 4.1. Official development assistance and conflict

Sustaining peace is a long-term pursuit that requires reliable and predictable financing. Furthermore, the sectoral allocation of ODA is equally important in promoting longer-term sustainable development outcomes. Therefore, it is imperative that determination of ODA deployment patterns factor in the twin objectives of strengthening socio-economic drivers and building peace, as the two are mutually supportive.

Available data suggest that a substantial volume of ODA does flow to conflict-stricken countries. Allocation patterns reveal that in the Asia-Pacific region, a significant share of ODA disbursements has gone to five countries with special needs that have been classified as high-risk and, in the case of Afghanistan, very high-risk (figure A).

Figure A. Official development assistance to Asia-Pacific countries with special needs, by INFORM risk class, 2007-2016

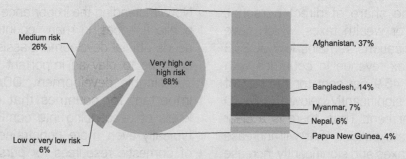

Source: ESCAP, based on data from OECD International Development Statistics. Available at stats.oecd.org/qwids. Accessed 21 March 2018.

Note: Risk classification is based on the 2018 INFORM scores.

While information and monitoring deficiencies limit an in-depth assessment of the alignment of ODA and conflict prevention priorities, a significant proportion of funding is channelled towards humanitarian activities, while an inadequate amount flows towards the goals of legitimate politics, security and justice (OECD, 2015). This pattern is slightly different in Asia and the Pacific, although countries with higher-risk levels do receive a higher percentage of humanitarian assistance when assessed relative to countries with lower-risk levels. Overall, an overwhelming proportion of ODA is allocated towards social infrastructure and services (figure B).

Figure B. Composition of official development assistance to Asia-Pacific countries with special needs, by INFORM risk class, 2007-2016

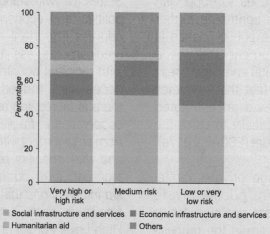

Source: ESCAP, based on data from OECD International Development Statistics. Available at stats.oecd.org/qwids. Accessed 21 March 2018.

Note: Risk classification is based on the 2018 INFORM scores.

Box 4.1. *(continued)*

The flow of ODA to high-risk countries or fragile States is also marked by a high degree of volatility, which is often a result of political decisions taken in donor countries rather than the outcome of long-term programming and planning (United Nations, 2015). In terms of sectorial allocation, limited ODA is channelled towards peace and security as well as conflict prevention purposes in Bangladesh, Myanmar and Papua New Guinea, which are each categorized as high-risk countries. This is consistent with findings that allocation towards such purposes spike only after large-scale conflict emerges.

One reason for this may be because conflicts and complementarities between the short-term goal of peace and the long-term goal of development are often poorly understood by donors (Boyce, 2008). Yet, there is an encouraging consensus emerging that building effective and legitimate governance structures is critical to sustaining peace and ensuring that countries do not fall back into violence (Boyce and Foreman, 2010). This requires resources and while initially they must be provided by the international community, in the longer-term building national fiscal capacities is critical for ensuring durable peace. Thus, development cooperation in fragile settings must also embed the priorities of enhancing domestic capacities to mobilize more resources in addition to laying the economic foundations for prosperity.

Given the complex multidimensional and multidirectional interplay between peace and the domains of sustainable development, an integrated and coherent approach that is cognizant of the linkages between these elements is critical to sustaining development in fragile, high-risk settings. Such an approach is already underway and represents a shift from previous arrangements when various dimensions of peace-building, including political, security and development objectives, were handled separately and conflict prevention was considered "nobody's business".

Ensuring ODA flows to countries that are currently exhibiting symptoms of fragility is critical to avoiding a delayed and costly response. Effectively, ODA must be aligned to the twin objectives of building strong foundations that minimize the "risk factors" of conflict while simultaneously fostering the institutional "conditions" to secure peace. Unfortunately, global trends reveal that international resources tend to be directed to post-conflict States while fragile States that are still on the cusp of conflict receive relatively little (Levin and Dollar, 2005). Perhaps donors prefer not to engage with countries they label as "difficult partnership" countries, due to the institutional shortcomings that may make the delivery of ODA and its implementation difficult. Despite these challenges, donors should not shy away from engaging with fragile countries. Rather, ODA to such States must be uniquely tailored to account for lower absorptive capacities and accountability standards.

that the channels of delivery or decision-making in such contexts are severely impaired, and that significant capacity deficiencies exist in human resource endowments.

Nevertheless, it is of concern therefore that flows of ODA continue to fall short of international commitments and that ODA continues to be fragmented. As the causes of conflict are multidimensional and require an integrated approach, streamlining ODA flows to fragile settings and enhancing synergies among donors is particularly important. Indeed, the structural and institutional impediments of high-risk countries warrant a more attuned approach to allocating and utilizing ODA.

At the highest multilateral level, the Addis Ababa Action Agenda on Financing for Development acknowledged *"the development challenge posed by conflict, which not only impedes but can reverse decades of development gains, [...] the peacebuilding financing gap, and the importance of the Peacebuilding Fund."*[2] Other encouraging developments, such as the New Deal for Engagement in Fragile States, also represent a shift that not only addresses the technical obstacles, but also the political obstacles to development progress.

F. The role of the international and regional organizations

International and regional organizations have an important role to play in preventing conflict and building peace. Responding to the call of the United Nations Secretary-General to address the root causes of conflict requires more focus on understanding and mitigating socio-economic risk drivers of conflict. This, includes research on areas related to sustaining peace, such as the effect of inequality of opportunities on sustainable development, equitable access to services and resources, building disaster resilience and ensuring macro-economic stability. More analytical work on the underlying causes of vulnerability of countries would draw attention to the impact of instability and conflict on sustainable development. Cooperation and knowledge exchange on field-tested policies for sustaining peace, preventing conflict and fostering sustainable development would be useful to policymakers in the region.

International and regional organizations can provide a vital coordination mechanism for analysing and mitigating risks related to conflict and crises. In addition to focusing analytical capacities on risks and drivers in certain risk hotspots, strategic partnerships with member Governments, the United Nations development agencies working on the ground, and peacekeeping or post-conflict transitional missions as well as selected agencies of the United Nations Country Teams would contribute to their work on sustaining peace and preventing conflict in the region.

Regional economic cooperation and integration, which contributes directly to the implementation of the 2030 Agenda for Sustainable Development, has a direct impact on sources of interstate conflict by strengthening confidence and trust between countries. At the same time, the enormous potential that exists for (a) generating trade, growth and employment as well as (b) improving social outcomes and managing environmental risks and shared vulnerabilities that closer cooperation and integration of economies offers, also contributes to sustaining peace and preventing conflict within countries. Countries within Asia and the Pacific, and especially countries with special needs, should therefore redouble their efforts to cooperate more closely within the region as well as integrate their economies.

ENDNOTES

[1] These estimates are for 2016 or latest available year, based on data from International Monetary Fund Government Finance Statistics and International Monetary Fund Article IV Consultation Reports.

[2] A/RES/69/313 para. 8.

ANNEX

Index for Risk Management and the threshold values used for risk classification, Asia-Pacific countries with special needs, 2018

COUNTRY	INFORM score	Risk class	Hazard and exposure	Natural	Human	Vulnerability	Socio-economic vulnerability	Vulnerable groups	Lack of coping capacity	Institutional	Infrastructure
Least developed countries	4.8		4.2	5.0	3.2	4.6	5.1	3.8	6.1	6.3	5.9
Afghanistan	7.7	Very High	8.7	6.0	10.0	7.1	6.4	7.7	7.5	7.2	7.8
Bangladesh	5.8	High	7.5	8.3	6.5	4.8	3.5	5.8	5.4	5.0	5.7
Bhutan	2.9	Low	1.8	3.2	0.2	2.9	4.3	1.2	4.6	4.2	5.0
Cambodia	4.7	Medium	4.8	5.5	4.0	3.4	3.8	3.0	6.5	7.0	6.0
Kiribati	3.6	Medium	1.6	2.9	0.1	4.9	6.1	3.3	6.1	6.0	6.1
Lao People's Democratic Republic	4.0	Medium	3.4	4.7	1.9	3.1	4.0	2.0	6.2	6.3	6.0
Myanmar	6.4	High	7.5	8.0	7.0	5.5	4.6	6.3	6.4	7.3	5.3
Nepal	5.1	High	5.4	5.5	5.3	4.2	3.8	4.6	5.9	6.3	5.5
Solomon Islands	4.8	Medium	3.4	5.3	0.8	4.9	7.2	1.3	6.6	6.6	6.5
Timor-Leste	4.2	Medium	2.6	3.8	1.3	4.2	4.8	3.6	6.6	6.6	6.6
Tuvalu	4.0	Medium	1.9	2.6	1.2	5.9	7.4	3.8	5.5	6.9	3.6
Vanuatu	3.9	Medium	2.3	4.0	0.1	4.3	5.2	3.2	6.1	6.0	6.2
Landlocked developoing countries	3.5		4.0	4.8	3.0	2.4	2.2	2.5	4.8	5.9	3.4
Armenia	3.6	Medium	3.3	4.2	2.2	3.0	2.4	3.6	4.9	6.8	2.3
Azerbaijan	4.7	Medium	5.0	4.5	5.4	4.5	1.5	6.5	4.7	6.3	2.5
Kazakhstan	2.2	Low	3.5	4.3	2.5	0.8	1.1	0.4	3.7	5.0	2.2
Kyrgyzstan	3.5	Medium	4.0	5.8	1.7	2.4	3.6	1.0	4.5	5.4	3.4
Mongolia	3.5	Medium	2.7	3.3	2.1	3.2	2.3	4.0	5.1	5.6	4.6
Tajikistan	4.4	Medium	5.7	6.0	5.4	3.0	2.8	3.1	5.1	5.9	4.1
Turkmenistan	2.7	Low	2.8	4.5	0.7	1.2	1.5	0.9	6.1	7.3	4.5
Uzbekistan	3.0	Low	5.0	6.1	3.6	1.3	2.0	0.6	4.1	4.9	3.3
Small island developing States	3.4		2.1	3.1	0.8	4.0	5.2	2.4	5.1	5.9	4.1
Fiji	3.1	Low	2.4	3.8	0.8	3.5	3.7	3.3	3.4	2.9	3.9
Maldives	2.3	Low	2.1	3.1	0.9	1.5	2.3	0.7	4.1	6.0	1.4
Marshall Islands	4.4	Medium	2.2	2.5	1.8	6.0	7.3	4.3	6.4	7.8	4.5
Micronesia (Federated States of)	4.1	Medium	2.2	3.7	0.3	5.3	6.5	3.7	5.8	5.9	5.6
Nauru	2.7	Low	0.8	1.4	0.1	4.5	5.7	3.1	5.6	7.1	3.6
Palau	2.7	Low	1.7	3.1	0.0	2.5	3.9	0.9	4.4	6.0	2.4
Papua New Guinea	5.5	High	4.3	5.3	3.2	5.2	5.7	4.6	7.6	6.7	8.3
Samoa	2.9	Low	1.6	2.7	0.3	3.4	5.5	0.4	4.3	4.5	4.0
Tonga	2.7	Low	1.2	2.2	0.1	3.7	5.8	0.8	4.6	5.8	3.2

Risk class	Threshold value										
Very high risk (>=)	6.5		6.1	6.9	9.0	6.4	7.1	6.3	7.6	7.3	7.4
High risk (>=)	5.0		4.1	4.7	7.0	4.8	5.4	4.4	6.0	6.0	5.4
Medium risk (>=)	3.5		2.7	2.8	3.1	3.2	3.5	2.9	4.7	4.9	3.5
Low risk (>=)	2.0		1.6	1.3	1.0	2.0	1.8	1.6	3.2	3.3	2.1
Very low risk (>=)	0.0		0.0	0.0	0.0	0.0	0.0	0.0	0.0	0.0	0.0

Source: Inter-Agency Standing Committee and the European Commissions. Available at www.inform-index.org. Accessed 20 November 2017.

REFERENCES

Acemoglu, Daron, Simon Johnson, and James A. Robinson (2001). The colonial origins of comparative development: An empirical investigation. *American Economic Review*, vol. 91, No. 5, pp. 1369-1401.

Annan, Kofi A. (2017). Towards a peaceful, fair and prosperous future for the people of Rakhine. Final report of the Advisory Commission on Rakhine State. Ministry of the Office of the State Counsellor of the Republic of the Union of Myanmar and the Kofi Annan Foundation.

Asian Development Bank (ADB) (2016). *Gender Statistics for the Pacific and Timor-Leste*. Manila.

Avalos, Nayda, Veronica Gonzales Stuva, Adam Heal, Kaoru Iida, and Naohito Okazoe (2015). Papua New Guinea and the natural resource curse. *Comparative Economic Studies*, vol. 57, No. 2, pp. 345-360.

Bahgat, Karim, Gray Barrett, Kendra Dupuy, Scott Gates, Solveig Hillesund, Havard Mokleiv Nygard, Siri Aas Rustad, Havard Strand, Henrik Urdal, and Gudrun Ostby (2017). Inequality and armed conflict: Evidence and data. Background Report for the United Nations and World Bank Flagship study on development and conflict prevention. Oslo: Peace Research Institute.

Bellemare, Marc F. (2015). Rising food prices, food price volatility, and social unrest. *American Journal of Agricultural Economics*, vol. 97, No. 1, pp. 1-21.

Besley, Timothy J., and Torsten Persson (2008). The incidence of civil war: Theory and evidence. National Bureau of Economic Research Working Paper No. 14585. Cambridge, MA, United States.

Blattman, Christopher, and Edward Miguel (2010). Civil war. *Journal of Economic Literature*, vol. 48, No. 1, pp. 3-57.

Blinov, Y. V. (2012). Ocenka vozdejstvija izmenenija klimata na vodnye resursy Kazahstana (Russian language). Background paper prepared for the Third-Sixth National Communication of the Republic of Kazakhstan to the Conference of Parties of the United Nations Framework Convention on Climate Change (UNFCCC). Unpublished manuscript.

Boyce, James K. (2008). Post-conflict recovery: Resource mobilization and reconstruction. Background paper prepared for United Nations Department of Economic and Social Affairs (DESA) Expert Group Meeting on Post-Conflict Recovery and Economic Insecurity, New York, 30 November 2017.

Boyce, James K., and Shepard Forman (2010). Financing peace: International and national resources for post conflict countries and fragile States. Background Paper for *World Development Report 2011*. Washington, D.C.: World Bank.

Brack, Duncan, and Gavin Hayman (2006). Managing trade in conflict resources, in Oli Brown, Mark Halle, Sonia Pena Moreno and Sebastian Winkler (eds.), *Trade, Aid and Security: An Agenda for Peace and Development*. Earthscan, London.

Brinkman, Henk-Jan, and Cullen S. Hendrix (2011). Food insecurity and violent conflict: Causes, consequences, and addressing the challenges. *Occasional Paper No. 24*. Rome: World Food Programme.

Burke, Marshall B., Edward Miguel, Shanker Satyanath, John A. Dykema, and David B. Lobell (2009). Warming increases the risk of civil war in Africa. *Proceedings of the National Academies of Sciences, Engineering, and Medicine*, vol. 106, No. 49, pp. 20670-20674.

Calì, Massimiliano, and Alen Mulabdic (2017). Trade and civil conflict: Revisiting the cross-country evidence. *Review of International Economics*, vol. 25, No. 1, pp. 195-232.

Chen, Siyan, Norman V. Loayza, and Marta Reynal-Querol (2008). The aftermath of civil war. *World Bank Economic Review*, vol. 22, No. 1, pp. 63-85. Washington, D.C.: World Bank.

Cho, Jaebeum, Alberto Isgut, and Yusuke Tateno (2016). An analytical framework for identifying optimal pathways towards sustainable development. Macroeconomic Policy and Financing for Development Division Working Paper Series No. WP/16/03. Bangkok: United Nations, Economic and Social Commission for Asia and the Pacific.

Cincotta, Richard P., Robert Engelman, and Daniele Anstasion (2003). *The Security Demographic: Population and Civil Conflict after the Cold War*. Washington, D.C.: Population Action International.

Collier, Paul (2007). *The Bottom Billion: Why the Poorest Countries Are Failing and What Can Be Done About It*. Oxford University Press.

Collier, Paul, Lani Elliott, Håvard Hegre, Anke Hoeffler, Marta Reynal-Queral, and Nicholas Sambanis (2003). *Breaking the Conflict Trap: Civil War and Development Policy*. World Bank Policy Research Report. Washington, D.C.: World Bank, and Oxford University Press.

Collier, Paul, and Anke Hoeffler (1998). On economic causes of civil war. *Oxford Economic Papers,* vol. 50, No. 4, pp. 563-573. Oxford University Press.

_____ (2004). Greed and grievance in civil war. *Oxford Economic Papers,* vol. 56, No 4, p. 563-595. Oxford University Press.

Cramer, Christopher (2010). Unemployment and participation in violence. Background paper for *World Development Report 2011.* World Bank: Washington, D.C.

De Nevers, Renée (1993). Democratization and Ethnic Conflict. *Survival,* vol. 35, No. 2, pp. 31-48.

Djankov, Simeon, and Marta Reynal-Querol (2010). Poverty and civil war: Revisiting the evidence. *The Review of Economics and Statistics,* vol. 92, No. 4, pp 1035-1041.

Do, Quy-Toan, and Lakshmi Iyer (2010). Geography, poverty and conflict in Nepal. *Journal of Peace Research,* vol. 47, No. 6, pp. 735-748.

Esteban, Joan Maria, and Debraj Ray (1994). On the measurement of polarization. *Econometrica,* vol. 62, No. 4, pp. 819-851.

Fearon, James D. (1995). Rationalist explanations for war. *International Organization,* vol. 49, No. 3, pp. 379-414.

_____ (2005). Primary commodity exports and civil war. *The Journal of Conflict Resolution,* vol. 49, No. 4, pp. 483-507.

Fearon, James D., and David D. Laitin (2003). Ethnicity, insurgency, and civil war. *American Political Science Review,* vol. 97, No. 1, pp. 75-90.

Ferris, Elizabeth (2010). Natural, disasters, conflict, and human rights: Tracing the connections. Presentation for the Brookings Institution–University of Bern Project on Internal Displacement. Washington, D.C.

Fjelde, Hanne (2015). Farming or fighting? Agricultural price shocks and civil war in Africa. *World Development,* vol. 67, pp. 525-534.

Gaibulloev, Khusrav, and Todd Sandler (2009). The impact of terrorism and conflicts on growth in Asia. *Economics & Politics,* vol. 21, No. 3, pp. 359-383.

Galtung, Johan (1996). *Peace by Peaceful Means: Peace and Conflict, Development and Civilization.* London: Sage Publications.

Garfinkel, Michelle R., and Stergios Skaperdas (2000). Conflict without misperceptions or incomplete information: How the future matters. *Journal of Conflict Resolution,* vol. 44, No. 6.

Ghani, Ejaz, and Lakshmi Iyer (2010). Conflict and development – lessons from South Asia. *Economic Premise,* No. 31. Washington, D.C.: World Bank.

Glantz, Michael H., and Igor S. Zonn (2005). *The Aral Sea: Water, Climate, and Environmental Change in Central Asia.* Geneva: World Meteorological Organization.

Government of Fiji (2016). *Fiji: Post-Disaster Needs Assessment: Tropical Cyclone Winston,* 20 February 2016.

Government of Kiribati (2016). *Kiribati Development Plan 2016-19: Towards a Better Educated, Healthier, More Prosperous Nation with a Higher Quality of Life.*

Government of Vanuatu (2015). *Vanuatu Post-Disaster Needs Assessment. Tropical Cyclone Pam,* March 2015.

Gurr, Ted Robert (1971). *Why Men Rebel.* Princeton University Press.

Hanks, Reuel R. (2010). *Global Security Watch - Central Asia.* Santa Barbara, California: Praeger.

Heinsohn, Gunnar (2003). *Söhne und Weltmacht: Terror im Aufstieg und Fall der Nationen.* Zürich.

Horowitz Donald L. (1985). *Ethnic Groups in Conflict.* University of California Press.

Hull, Peter, and Masami Imai (2013). Economic shocks and civil conflict: Evidence from foreign interest rate movements. *Journal of Development Economics,* No. 103, pp. 77-89.

Huntington, Samuel (1993). The clash of civilizations? *Foreign Affairs,* vol. 72, No. 3, pp. 22-49.

Hsiang, Solomon M., Marshall Burke, and Edward Miguel (2013). Quantifying the influence of climate on human conflict. *Science,* 10.1126/science.1235367.

Ibatullin, Saghit (2013). Water resources in Central Asia: Current status, problems and perspectives of use. Unpublished manuscript.

Institute for Economics and Peace (2017). *The 2017 Global Peace Index.* Sydney, Australia: IEP.

Inter-Agency Standing Committee and the European Commission. Inform Global Risk Index: Results 2018. Available at www.inform-index.org.

Isham, Jonathan, Michael Woolcock, Lant Pritchett, and Gwen Busby (2005). The varieties of resource experience: Natural resource export structures and the political economy of economic growth. *World Bank Economic Review*, vol. 19, No. 2, p. 141-174.

Iyer, Lakshmi, and Indhira Santos (2012). Creating jobs in South Asia's conflict zones. Policy Research Working Paper No. 6104. Washington, D.C.: World Bank.

Kanbur, Ravi (2007). Poverty and conflict: The inequality link. Coping with Crisis Working Paper Series. Vienna: International Peace Academy.

Kim, Namsuk, and Pedro Conceição (2010). The economic crisis, violent conflict, and human development. *International Journal of Peace Studies*, vol. 25, No. 1, 21-43.

Kim, Namsuk, and Melanie Sauter (2017). Is conflict an additional structural obstacle for least developed countries? *International Journal of Development and Conflict*, vol. 7, No. 1, pp. 32-48.

La Ferrara, Eliana, and Robert H. Bates (2001). Political competition in weak States. CID Working Paper No. 68, Center for International Development, Harvard University.

Levin, Victoria, and David Dollar (2005). The forgotten States: Aid volumes and volatility in difficult partnership countries (1992-2002). Summary paper prepared for the Development Assistance Committee Learning and Advisory Process on Difficult Partnerships.

Looney, Robert (2006). Economic consequences of conflict: The rise of Iraq's informal economy. *Journal of Economic Issues*, vol. 40, No. 4, pp. 991-1007.

Mansfield, Edward D., and Jack Snyder (1995). Democratization and the danger of war. *International Security*, vol. 20, No. 1, pp. 5-38.

Mazo, Jeffrey (2010). *Climate Conflict: How Global Warming Threatens Security and What to Do about It*. Routledge. ISBN: 978-0-415-59118-8.

McBride, Michael, and Stergios Skaperdas (2007). Explaining conflict in low-income countries: Incomplete contracting in the shadow of the future, in M. Gradstein and K. Konrad (Eds.), *Institutions and Norms in Economic Development*, MIT Press, Cambridge: MA.

Melander, Erik, Therese Pettersson, and Lotta Themner (2016). Organized violence, 1989-2015. *Journal of Peace Research*, vol. 53, No. 5, pp. 727-742.

Mobjörk, Malin, Maria-Therese Gustafsson, Hannes Sonnsjö, Sebastian van Baalen, Lisa Maria Dellmuth, and Niklas Bremberg (2016). *Climate-Related Security Risks: Towards an Integrated Approach*. Stockholm International Peace Research Institute.

North, Douglass C. (2006). *Understanding the Process of Economic Change*. Princeton: Princeton University Press.

Organisation for Economic Co-operation and Development (OECD) (2015). *States of Fragility 2015: Meeting Post-2015 Ambitions*. Paris: OECD Publishing.

Ovadiya, Mirey, Adea Kryeziu, Syeda Masood, and Eric Zapatero (2015). Social protection in fragile and conflict-affected countries: Trends and challenges. Social Protection and Labour Discussion Paper No. 1502. Washington, D.C.: World Bank.

Pereira, Natalia (2011). Return[ed] to paradise: The deportation experience in Samoa and Tonga. UNESCO Policy Papers No. 21. Paris: United Nations Educational, Scientific and Cultural Organisation.

Piketty, Thomas (2014). *Capital in the Twenty-First Century*. Arthur Gold hammer, trans. Belknap Press, Harvard University Press. Cambridge.

Political Instability Task Force (2017). State Failure Problem Set. Center for Systemic Peace, Vienna VA, United States. Available at http://www.systemicpeace.org/inscrdata.html.

Powell, Martin (2006). Social policy and administration: Journal and discipline. *Social Policy and Administration*, vol. 40, No. 3, pp. 233-249.

Rajkumar, Andrew Sunil, and Vinaya Swaroop (2008). Public spending and outcomes: Does governance matter? *Journal of Development Economics*, vol. 86, pp. 96-111.

Rauchhaus, Robert W. (2006). Asymmetric information, mediation, and conflict management. *World Politics*, vol. 58, No. 2, pp. 207-241.

Ray, Debraj (2009). Remarks on the initiation of costly conflict. Paper presented at the Yale University Workshop on Rationality and Conflict, New Haven, United States.

Ray, Debraj, and Joan Maria Esteban (2017). Conflict and development. *The Annual Review of Economics*, vol. 9, pp. 263-293.

Reilly, Benjamin (2002). Internal conflict and regional security in Asia and the Pacific. *Pacifica Review*, vol. 14, No. 1.

Ross, Michael (2004). How do natural resources influence civil war? Evidence from thirteen cases. *International Organization*, vol. 58, No. 1, pp. 35-67.

_____ (2006). A closer look at oil, diamonds, and civil war. *Annual Review of Political Science*, vol. 9, pp. 265-300.

_____ (2015). What have we learned about the resource curse? *Annual Review of Political Science*, vol. 18, pp. 239-259.

Sachs, Jeffrey D., and Andrew M. Warner (1995). Natural resource abundance and economic growth, National Bureau of Economic Research Working Paper No. 5398. Cambridge, MA, United States.

Skaperdas, Stergios (2008). An economic approach to analyzing civil wars. *Economics of Governance*, vol. 9, No. 1, pp. 25-44.

Smith, Alan (2010). The influence of education on conflict and peace building. Background paper prepared for the Education for all Global Monitoring Report 2011 - *The Hidden Crisis: Armed Conflict and Education*. Paris: United Nations Educational, Scientific and Cultural Organization.

Solow, Robert M. (1991). Sustainability: an economist's perspective. Paper presented at the Eighteenth J. Seward Johnson Lecture to the Marine Policy Center, Woods Hotel Oceanographic Institution, Woods Hotel, Massachusetts, 14 June 1991.

Stewart, Frances (2000). Crisis prevention: Tackling horizontal inequalities. *Oxford Development Studies*, vol. 28, No. 3, pp. 245-262.

Suleimenova, Zulfiya (2018). Water security in Central Asia and the Caucasus – A key to peace and sustainable development. Background paper prepared for the *Asia-Pacific Countries with Special Needs Development Report 2018*. Bangkok: ESCAP.

Swaine, Michael D., Nicholas Eberstadt, M. Taylor Fravel, Mikkal Herberg, Albert Keidel, Evans J. R. Revere, Alan D. Romberg, Eleanor Freund, Rachel Esplin Odell, and Audrye Wong (2015). *Conflict and Cooperation in the Asia-Pacific Region: A Strategic Net Assessment*. Washington, D.C.: Carnegie Endowment for International Peace.

The Asia Foundation (2016). *Annual Report 2016: Addressing the Critical Issues Facing Asia*. San Francisco, United States.

_____ (2017). *The State of Conflict and Violence in Asia*. Bangkok.

United Nations (2015). Improving ODA allocations for a post-2015 world: Targeting aid to benefit the poorest 20% of people in developing countries. Background paper prepared for the 2016 Development Cooperation Forum. United Nations Department of Economic and Social Affairs (DESA), New York, Development Initiatives, Bristol, United Kingdom, and UK Aid. Available at http://www.un.org/en/ecosoc/newfunct/pdf15/un_improving_oda_allocation_for_post-2015_world.pdf.

United Nations, and World Bank (2017). *Pathways for Peace: Inclusive Approaches to Preventing Violent Conflict - Main Messages and Emerging Policy Directions*. United Nations, New York, and World Bank, Washington D.C.

United Nations Development Programme (UNDP) (2008). Armed violence in Asia and the Pacific: An overview of the Causes, Costs and Consequences. Briefing paper. New York.

_____ (2015). *Labour Migration, Remittances, and Human Development in Central Asia*. Central Asia Human Development Series. Eurasian Development Bank, Almaty, and UNDP, New York.

_____ (2016a). *Asia-Pacific Human Development Report: Shaping the future: How changing demographics can power human development*. New York.

_____ (2016b). *UNDP support to the implementation of the 2030 Agenda for Sustainable Development*. New York.

United Nations Environmental Programme (UNEP) (2007). *Sudan: post-conflict environmental assessment*. Nairobi.

United Nations Interagency Framework Team for Preventive Action (2012). *Land and conflict: Toolkit and guidance for preventing and managing land and natural resources conflict*. New York.

United Nations, Economic and Social Commission for Asia and the Pacific (ESCAP) (2015). *Asia-Pacific Countries with Special Needs Development Report 2015: Building Productive Capacities to Overcome Structural Challnges*. Sales No. E.15.II.F.9.

_____ (2016). *Asia-Pacific Countries with Special Needs Development Report 2016: Adapting the 2030 Agenda for Sustainable Development at the National Level*. Sales No. E.16.II.F.11.

_____ (2017a). *Asia-Pacific Countries with Special Needs Development Report 2017: Investing in infrastructure for an inclusive and sustainable future*. Sales No. E.17.II.F.9.

_____ (2017b). *Economic and Social Survey of Asia and the Pacific 2017: Governance and Fiscal Management*. Sales No. E.17.IIF.2.

_____ (2017c). *Gender, the Environment and Sustainable Development in Asia and the Pacific.* Sales No. E.17.II.F.18.

_____ (2017d). Natural disasters and conflict in Asia-Pacific: Issues of co-relation and contiguity. Unpublished manuscript.

_____ (2017e). *Sustainable Social Development in Asia and the Pacific: Towards a people-centred transformation.* Sales No. E.17.II.F.15.

_____ (2018). Inequality of Opportunity in Asia and the Pacific. Social Development Policy Papers. Available at http://www.unescap.org/our-work/social-development/poverty-and-inequality/resources.

United Nations, Economic and Social Commission for Asia and the Pacific (ESCAP), Asian Development Bank (ADB), and United Nations Development Programme (UNDP) (2017). *Asia-Pacific Sustainable Development Goals Outlook.* ESCAP, Bangkok; ADB, Manila; and UNDP, New York.

United Nations, Office of the High Representative for the Least Developed Countries, Landlocked Developing Countries and Small Island Developing States (OHRLLS) (2013). Effective support for fragile and post-conflict least developed countries: Fragility as a development challenge. Available at: http://unohrlls.org/custom-content/uploads/2013/09/Effective-support-for-fragile-and-post_conflict.pdf.

Uppsala Conflict Data Program (UCDP). Available at http://ucdp.uu.se/.

Urdal, Henrik (2004). The devil in the demographics: The effect of youth bulges on domestic armed conflict, 1950-2000. *Social Development Papers: Conflict Prevention and Reconstruction No. 14.* Washington, D.C.: World Bank.

Weinberg, Joe, and Ryan Bakker (2015). Let them eat cake: Food prices, domestic policy and social unrest. *Conflict Management and Peace Science,* vol. 32, No. 3.

Whish-Wilson, Phillip (2002). The Aral Sea environmental health crisis. *Journal of Rural and Remote Environmental Health,* vol. 1, No. 2, pp. 29-34.

World Health Organization (WHO) (2001). *The World Health Report 2001 - Mental Health: New Understanding, New Hope.* Geneva.

World Bank (2011). *World Development Report 2011: Conflict, Security, and Development.* Washington, D.C.

_____ (2013). *Catastrophe Risk Assessment Methodology.* Washington, D.C.

_____ (2016). Migration and remittances: Recent developments and outlook. *Migration and Development Brief,* No. 26. Washington, D.C.

_____ (2017). *World Development Report 2017: Governance and the Law.* Washington, D.C.

Yilmaz, Muzaffer Ercan (2007). Intra-state conflicts in the post-cold war era. *International Journal on World Peace,* vol. 24, No. 4, pp. 11-33.

Zasloff, Joseph J. (2002). Emerging stability in Cambodia, *Asian Affairs,* vol. 28, No. 4, pp. 187-200.